HURRY LESS  WORRY LESS
FOR FAMILIES

Other Abingdon Press Books by Judy Christie

Hurry Less, Worry Less
Hurry Less, Worry Less at Christmastime
Hurry Less, Worry Less at Work
Goodbye, Murphy's Law: Whatever Can Go Wrong,
    God Can Make Right
Awesome Altars, with Mary Dark

Fiction:

Gone to Green
Goodness Gracious Green (available Fall 2010)

HURRY LESS WORRY LESS
for
FAMILIES

JUDY CHRISTIE

Abingdon Press
Nashville

HURRY LESS, WORRY LESS FOR FAMILIES

Copyright © 2010 by Abingdon Press

This book is printed on acid-free paper.

Library of Congress Cataloging-in-Publication Data

Christie, Judy Pace, 1956–
  Hurry less, worry less for families / Judy Christie.
    p. cm.
  ISBN 978-0-687-65914-2 (pbk. - : alk. paper)
  1. Families—Religious life. 2. Time management—Religious aspects—Christianity. 3. Peace of mind—Religious aspects—Christianity. I. Title.
  BV4526.3.C47 2010
  248.8'45—dc22
                                                        2009048094

10 11 12 13 14 15 16 17 18 19 — 10 9 8 7 6 5 4 3 2 1

MANUFACTURED IN THE UNITED STATES OF AMERICA

To our new family members,

Caroline and Finn;

and their wonderful parents,

Jeff, Katherine, Ryan, and Tiffany

CONTENTS

WITH GRATITUDE

I offer my heartfelt thanks to the many parents who so generously offered wise and candid thoughts for this book. The words *thank you* sound too puny to sum up my gratitude. More than one hundred mothers and fathers gave their real-life family insights to help shape the pages that follow, enduring lengthy interviews and multiple follow-up questions. A handful of young people, from elementary school to college, also provided their perspectives. In respect for their families' privacy, I did not use their names, but each of them will notice their influence.

This awesome group included professionals in the world of child development, loving members of the Pace-Christie clans, spectacular folks in my church family at Grace Community United Methodist Church, and Baylor FunFest Friends. And I don't know where I would be without Alisa Stingley, who edits and suggests; and my agent, Etta Wilson, who keeps me on track.

I must say a special thanks to Suzanne, who was the first to answer my parenting questions and who is such a great mom to grandaughter Gracie, and to our wonderful son-in-law, Tony, who adds so much to our family.

With Gratitude

I could not write a book about family without calling upon the memory of my parents, Charlie and Betty Pace, who started me on the right path.

Finally, as always, my love and thanks go to my husband, Paul, who somehow puts up with my book deadlines and helps make our family life so much fun.

INTRODUCTION

"See, I have placed before you an open door that no one can shut."—Revelation 3:8

*I*t's like a pop quiz every day."

That is the way one young mother has described busy parenting.

Other parents are quick to agree.

"Parenthood has been both the hardest job I ever tackled and the most rewarding."

"Trial and error."

"The most important position, role, and responsibility I have ever had."

I've never seen a subject where individuals are so quick to admit they often do not get it right, a topic where people so earnestly want to be better and are so certain that others are superior. Nor have I seen another topic that has a more consistent impact on the world!

Other themes quickly emerge in conversations with parents: Mom and Dad try to balance work, home, church, and community involvement. Children have a steady stream of activities. Outside demands result in inside friction. Parents and siblings grow older, and they begin to need a different kind of time and attention. People want to have more fun with their children. Families splinter, and people remarry. Mothers and fathers sheepishly tell stories of the missteps they have taken, and they search for more time for themselves and with their mates.

In this book, we'll walk through those issues and explore simple steps to deal with them. I have met thousands of people who seek a fulfilling, happy life with their families. This is a learning process and a rich and challenging journey. I pray that the candid and thoughtful comments of scores of parents offered here will spark your own ideas and conversations.

These pages offer tools to shape the family life you want, whatever stage of life you are in, and to explore answers to layers of questions. Each chapter includes comments from families for you to consider, questions about your unique family, a prayer for your journey, and useful tips from busy parents. You'll see the words of mothers and fathers who are trying hard and who know how tough and wonderful family life is, as well as insights from everyone from young children to retired adults.

Be assured that there are no perfect families. But there are successes in the lives of many who step forward with faith, hope, and love. They have learned not to give up when they stumble. My wish is that you'll recognize many of those achievements in your own family and borrow new ways to move forward.

You already have the pieces you need in order to make needed changes. You don't have to shoot for perfection. Each family has challenges. You can find answers for your family and customize a plan that works for you and yours. God wants everyday people to live fully, to enjoy life. Our families offer a base camp for learning to do just that.

The hardest part may be believing that change is possible. No matter the ages of your children or the details of your family, you can begin to change, to enjoy each day more.

Consider your unique life, your one-of-a-kind family. Give yourself credit for what you have done right, and consider how to continue to improve.

Say a prayer asking God to guide you. Decide to take steps to make needed changes. Know that divine plans are in place for you and your family. May you find much family fun along the way. May you have strength and courage to deal with difficulties. May you be aware of God's love surrounding you and your family.

Do not hesitate to walk through the door before you. You may not make a perfect score on the "pop quiz" of family life or parenting. But you can change the world through your efforts.

Chapter One

A FRESH LOOK
AT YOUR FAMILY

Encouraging Word: *Your family life can be more joyful.*
Everyday Step: *Give thanks for your family each morning.*

"Ask and it will be given to you; seek and you will find;
knock and the door will be opened to you."
—Luke 11:9

*T*he long carpool line at school winds out into the street
and parents politely wait their turn while impatiently looking
at their watches. Adults talk on cell phones while waiting for
children to appear, masters at whipping into the drive at just
the right moment.

From school it's off to dance or soccer or art or guitar lessons, or you name the activity. Some people zoom between
multiple schools. Parents juggle work schedules to pick up
and deliver. They coordinate rides with the precision of an
army general, depending on neighbors, family, after-school
programs, and prayers to handle the logistics. Some families
practically live out of their cars. And this is just part of a typ-
ical busy day. By the time the weekend rolls around, everyone is worn out and trying to figure out how to fit everything
into the Saturday and Sunday schedules.

Shaping a loving, contented family is probably the most important job you will ever have, and perhaps the most challenging. Being part of a loving family adds richness to your world. Leading a loving family is both an honor and a gift. You may feel blessed beyond belief at the joy of your children, and scared, on some days, that you are not up to the job.

To hurry less and worry less as a family, you must:

- Decide what is most important to you.
- Make daily decisions that support those priorities.
- Adjust as needed.

You can't do it just once; you have to try again each day. But the great thing about that is that you get new chances every day. Thank goodness!

Most parents know what they want. They are hungry for their children to know they are loved. They want happiness for their families and to help their children recognize what is truly important in life. They watch eagerly to see how their kids develop and try to give them what they need to be safe and healthy.

That is the Big Picture.

Then come the details of each day. Those can be tough.

Teaching children requires consistency and commitment. You must try to make good decisions each day, decisions that support dreams, goals, and priorities for your family.

As you take a fresh look, consider daily steps that can help you reach your goals. Often these are little things, such as sitting with your child on the floor laughing at a game, playing catch in the yard, or avoiding an evening meeting to have supper together as a family. Small actions can yield big changes.

Ask. Seek. Knock.

Guidance and wisdom are needed, each and every day, to help your children become the people they were created to be. Some moments will be joyful and seem easy. Others will call upon every ounce of patience and resolve you have, and they will surprise you with their force. Along the way you have to dig deep to do your best and forgive yourself when you falter.

To identify what is most important for your family, turn to God. **Ask:** for support in shaping your family. "Help us, Lord!" **Seek:** divine instruction. Seeking is a process, not a one-time-only deal. Life unfolds in unexpected ways. **Knock:** on the door every single day, inviting God's divine awareness in your life. Don't be distracted by your flaws or weaknesses. Ask God for forgiveness, and say thanks for the gift of your family.

Accept Yourself

Perhaps you try hard every day but feel as though you are in a big muddy bog. You hit the ground running in the morning and scarcely slow down until you fall into bed exhausted.

Many moms and dads grade themselves harshly. But ease up on yourself. Sure, you have made mistakes. But you have done many things well and can build on those successes.

Perfect parents do not exist, so you do not have to try to be one.

- Assess both what you have done well and what you would like to change.
- Consider how to do things better, starting now.

3

- Fast forward: for example, picture a family milestone you anticipate, such as a child's high school graduation, a daughter's or son's wedding, or your child's first job. What do you want your children to carry with them into these times? What might you do now to help them find their way?

- Think anew about what you want your children to remember about childhood. What are the lessons you want to impart, starting now? You can make changes no matter the ages of your children.

- Consider your philosophy of parenting and how you came up with it.

As one father says: "I want my children to remember the happy times and feel like they were loved, nurtured, and appreciated for the individuals they are. We have tried so hard to provide that kind of environment. I do not want their collective experience to be based on material things, but instead to be based on love and understanding."

What do you want for *your* family?

Setting the Pace

The tone for families comes from parents. Your approach will have a long-lasting impact. "Parents definitely set the pace," says a Texas family counselor. "If you are stressed, it carries over to the family. Children learn some of their coping skills from parents."

Teach your children, through your words and deeds, to be calm and relaxed. Help them learn to solve problems and face the hard parts of life.

Take a Fresh Look

One of the most important things you can do is to pause from time to time, identify goals and dreams for your home and your family, and then step back for a few minutes to assess.

You know how easy it is to get so wrapped up in "doing" everyday life that you don't stop to consider what you might do differently. Carefully answering questions about goals can shift your approach to family life. It's amazing to watch this happen.

Think about what is most important for *your* family. This will help clear out unimportant matters, those little things that drain you and hold you back. Be specific. Customize goals, and don't try to make your family look like someone else's.

First the What, Then the How

As you consider hurrying less and worrying less with your family, begin to identify what you want and what you do *not* want. When you know what you want, you can begin to figure out how to get it.

This is a tried-and-true strategy: first the what, then the how.

You do not have to start from scratch, organize a family retreat, or come up with a bound volume of family values. Instead, consider basic questions:

How would you describe your enjoyable family life?

What steps are you taking to help shape it that way?

No matter what ages your children are, how do you want them to feel about home and family?

These questions can raise fears. You may second-guess yourself on not having done well enough or started soon enough. You may even worry that children in other families have better lives or kinder parents or a more creative home.

But stop. You are doing many things right!

As you search for strategies in your life, remember the ancient parenting manual, the Bible. God's word is full of stories of families, both good and bad, and it contains parenting advice that has withstood the test of the ages. Woven throughout the Bible is the message of God's special plans for each individual, a reminder of the responsibility of wise parenting. "Jesus said, 'Let the little children come to me, and do not stop them; for it is to such as these that the kingdom of heaven belongs'" (Matthew 19:14 NRSV). This is a reminder that what you are doing does indeed matter.

Getting Started

So here you sit.

You have the best intentions. You know you want to make changes. But you can't get off dead center.

Perhaps you are in a rut with your family, doing the same things all the time and not being satisfied with how that feels. Maybe job demands or money worries or health challenges distract you. You realize you have not thought enough about the kind of parent you want to be or considered small changes you could make for big rewards.

Often in our busy lives, we have trouble getting started. The big task or goal seems overwhelming, so we do nothing. Procrastination only adds to our burdens and makes us tired.

Take a deep breath and plunge in, and do not expect to do everything at once.

You may often come up against the expectations of others—demands from your own parents and friends, requests from church and civic groups, and others. To wisely deal with these conflicts requires knowing what you want for your family and making daily decisions accordingly.

Keep bringing yourself back to what is most important: your priorities. It would be nice if you could list these priorities once, and that would be that. But you have to keep focusing on them.

Consider the verse from Romans 12:2, a favorite passage for shaping a less-hurried and less-worried life: "Do not conform any longer to the pattern of this world, but be transformed by the renewing of your mind. Then you will be able to test and approve what God's will is—his good, pleasing and perfect will." When most families around you are hurried and worried, they will expect you to act likewise. You can begin to change the world when you show a different way of living through your own family. Think of the power of your little brood influencing the people you encounter and transforming the world.

A mother on the East Coast has made a conscious effort to slow her family down and to have rich, calm time with her husband and three children. "My biggest challenge is that other people want us to be busy," she says. "Our society from all aspects is telling us we must be doing this and that, and that we aren't really being productive if we are not filling every moment with something."

Imagine how your priorities look in daily life. Be as specific as possible. Once you begin to see your priorities in your mind, you will begin to appreciate more fully why they matter. What activities will you need to stop doing in order to focus on those that really are important to you?

Almost without exception, families *hurry* too much and want to spend more time together. So "hurry less" can be a basic goal, with "having fun family time" as a priority.

Next, parents *worry*. They are fearful and lose sleep over

their children. Perhaps you need "worry less" as a goal, with "solving nagging problems" as a priority.

Finally, parents tend to expect the worst. Most people live by Murphy's Law, believing that whatever can go wrong will go wrong. Maybe you want to be more optimistic or hopeful in your family, with "creating an encouraging home life" as a goal.

Shape a Philosophy of Parenting

Different people have different approaches to parenting. Some have a specific philosophy, while others have a general idea. Your parenting philosophy needs to suit the vision you have for your family and your life.

Maybe you drifted into where you are. Maybe you were strategic. Perhaps you are among those mothers and fathers who know what they want for their children and who try to make decisions accordingly. Or perhaps you are a bit unsure. **Decide what works for your family, and build upon that.**

- One mother in her twenties sums up her philosophy of parenting in one word: "simple." She explains: "I like my life to be as simplified as possible, so it came naturally to do the same in raising my child."
- Another parent has a similar view. "I work from the future back," she says. "I know what I want for my children's future, and I always frame my decisions around that. And I always try to keep the idea that my role is to be their parent, and my job is to give them the tools to do well in life, and I try not to worry about the things I shouldn't worry about."
- A busy father of three sons says he and his wife apply the "divide and conquer" philosophy to parenting. "It

takes teamwork and strategy to get all tasks accomplished and to keep everyone in sync. We both sacrifice less-important things to make sure that more-important things are taken care of."

- A teacher who is a single parent says that she wants to teach her children to make good choices. This guides her parenting style. She uses that goal to keep the family from being on the go all the time. "I don't overschedule. It's important not to just *do* and *do* and *do* all the time. It's up to us as parents to figure it out."

As you step back, use prayer to help. Offer thanks for the joys and distractions, for your children, your parents, and all those in your family, for the way each day comes together. Ask God for help, for wisdom and patience, and for direction in matters large and small. Surrender concerns to God, knowing that the Creator's power will sustain you.

Remember: Ask. Seek. Knock.

One working mother puts her house slippers a few feet away from her bed. As she walks over to them each morning, she prays, building the habit with which she wants to start every day. Do whatever works for you!

Accept parenting as a fun and challenging journey. You have an important mission with your family, and challenges are part of it. Keep that in perspective.

Even Christ's parents faced challenges. Remember their annual trip to Jerusalem for Passover, when Christ was a boy? When the festival ended and they started to return home, twelve-year-old Jesus stayed behind in Jerusalem, but his parents did not know it. Assuming that he was somewhere among them in the large group of travelers, they went a day's journey. Then they started to look for him among their relatives and friends. When they did not find him, they returned to Jerusalem to search for him. After three days they found Jesus in the temple, "sitting among the teachers, listening to them and asking them questions" (Luke 2:46).

I can picture the scene—the annual trip, the preparations, the commotion, and the parents assuming that Jesus was somewhere with the group. Can't you just imagine the panic when they realized their son was not around and were unable to find him for three days?

It is hard to get it right all the time.

Consider this parent's words, and see if they sound familiar at all: "There is no magic answer. We struggle daily to maintain a proper balance. We try (and sometimes fail) to keep God at the forefront of what we do—stressing to our kids the importance of faithfulness and harmony. I don't feel like we do a great job of balancing; we struggle just like everyone else. We certainly make plenty of parenting mistakes, but I feel like our kids are well adjusted despite the hectic nature of our family and professional lives. We have had to come up with our style on our own, each borrowing pieces of what worked in our personal lives growing up."

Do you wish for a magic answer? Are you trying to find what works for you?

Families are different. Shape what works for you.

"I believe our children are gifts from God. They belong to God. We are answering the call of service for his children," says a longtime director in children's ministry and the mom of young children. "I believe our children should be raised in a loving, faith-filled environment balanced with respect for both parent and child. With the love comes discipline, which doesn't always mean punishment, but a way to be respectful, trustworthy, caring, educating, responsible human beings."

Some families have Mom and Dad together. Some homes are led by one parent after a divorce or the death of a spouse, which can make it even more difficult to juggle schedules. Some parents work outside the home, while some have a full-time job working inside the home. Some families are noisy, and others quiet. One parent may love the outdoors, while another may prefer indoor games and reading. Some welcome travel, while others like to stay put. Families come in so many forms these days—with varied circumstances—and we need not expect ours to look like the family next door. Our families are different, and we can give thanks for that as we look to God for guidance.

How about your family? "One size fits all" does not work when it comes to making big life decisions and setting goals.

Family Concerns

For all of the differences between parents, most of them share certain concerns:

- Am I spending enough time with my family?
- Are my children getting what they need?
- Are my children developing and growing at a normal pace?
- Will my children be successful and happy?
- Am I being a good role model for them?
- Will I be able to provide for them financially?

Don't fret that other families may seem to do better than yours. Comparing yourself to others is often discouraging. You begin to believe that everyone else does things just a little better than you. Maybe you wince to think how people would feel if they saw your family in an unguarded moment. Each family has challenges, setbacks, victories, and meaningful moments.

Parents put such high expectations on themselves that a Super-Ultra Parent of the Year could not meet all of them. The director of a highly regarded child development center, who is the mother of a young child, says: "The biggest challenge for me is probably reassuring myself that I am doing all that I can and that I am doing the right things while parenting. The biggest challenge, therefore, is living up to the expectations that I put on myself."

And consider this comment from another parent: "You've got to learn to forgive yourself. There will be times as a parent when we make mistakes and say the wrong thing."

Give up guilt. Many parents add guilt to their already heavy loads. They fret about mistakes they have made, the amount of time they don't spend with their children, their attitude, or their actions. Guilt drains your energy. Decide instead to pray when you feel guilty, to relinquish your shortcomings, and to look for small ways to move forward.

Just about everyone wishes he or she could be a better parent, that his or her family could be more "together," and that he or she was wiser. In visiting at length with more than one hundred parents for this book, I did not come across one parent who thought that he or she had it all figured out. No matter where you are on your parenting journey, you're in good company.

Making the Best Decisions

A devoted mother, with a demanding job and a husband whose work took him out of state for lengthy periods of time, is one of many parents who discussed her desire to have a close relationship with her children while making hard decisions: "I want them to know that what we do is for a reason, with the bigger picture in mind, their future and ability to function as a successful parent and member of society one day, to be a good friend, respected by others, who can make a difference in other people's lives. My children don't like me all the time. So a challenge for me is not always making the popular decisions, but making the best decisions I can as a parent. Another challenge is not looking back at parenting mistakes, but to continue to move ahead and learn from my mistakes. Parenting is the most difficult job I have ever taken on in my life, and it is as much a learning process for me as it is for my children. Luckily, it is not a challenge to love my children with every ounce of my being and to let them know all the time that whatever they do, I will never stop loving them."

You may feel the same way. You grow and learn and get better as you go. This process is full of hope. You have the chance to tweak and overhaul and change. You can do better tomorrow and learn from what you did yesterday and today. You are given fresh starts, new chances.

A Step or Two

- List what you love about your family life.
- List what you would like to change.
- Jot down a half-dozen small steps to begin to make needed changes. Don't try to change the world in a day.
- Take a deep breath and smile. You are on your way!

Questions to Consider as You Go Forward

- How would you describe your philosophy of parenting?
- How did you decide on your approach to parenting?
- What would you like to change?

A PRAYER FOR YOUR JOURNEY

Dear God, thank you for loving me and for helping me love my family. Please show me the right steps to take, and help me make wise decisions. Guide me as I try to be faithful and loving, and as I make hard choices for those I care about. Watch over my family, and help each member know your love; in the name of Christ. Amen.

Observations from Busy Families

"I have been told over and over that the girls will grow up before I know it, and to enjoy them while I can. This is so very true. The time spent hurrying around to be at everything and to buy everything and to worry about everything can never be recouped. It's gone forever, and before you know it, they don't want to hold your hand when walking across the street, and they don't want to spend the evening curled up in your bed or without their cell phone or iPods. Really grab that time together every chance you get."

"Spend time with them. Hold them. Love them. Teach them right from wrong. Teach them to laugh."

"Be sure to make time to have quality time. With so many activities that families have to do, having a set schedule that cannot be broken is important. We know a company president who keeps a standing Tuesday night date with his family to go bowling."

Quick Tip

"Make time to really listen to children, and get down to their eye level when you speak to them, as well as when they are speaking."

Chapter Two

ENOUGH TIME TO GO AROUND

Encouraging Word: *No matter how busy you are, you can slow down.*
Everyday Step: *Cut something from today's schedule.*

Yet this I call to mind / and therefore I have hope: / Because of the LORD's great love we are not consumed, / for his compassions never fail. / They are new every morning.
—Lamentations 3:21-23a

A dense fog settled upon our neighborhood as the weather changed. Out for a morning walk, I was unable to see more than a few inches in front of me. Familiar landmarks completely disappeared. I gingerly made my way, taking one careful step after another, trying to stay on the path.

Almost imperceptibly, the fog lifted. The view ahead grew clearer for a few feet and then a few yards. The way was now obvious.

Sometimes parenting feels like this. Your way is blurred, your path obscured. You may be on a familiar path, one you have traveled for years, and suddenly find yourself lost. You are not quite sure what to do or how to do it. Every day, new decisions arise. The challenges of life press in.

On a regular basis, check out your parenting footing. Consider what works in your family life and what needs tweaking. Ponder what might be getting lost in the fog of everyday life. Savor the knowledge that God's mercies are new every day, and that each day brings a fresh opportunity to you as a parent to find enough time to do what you need to do.

Part of slowing down as a family includes taking a hard look at how each family member spends his or her time and deciding what activities might need to go. Without your realizing it, a heavy fog of overdoing it can settle around your family.

In deciding how to use your time, consider the must-do items, such as homework, and figure out how much wiggle room there is in your day. Think again of how you want your family life to feel. Use this to guide choices.

The buzz of family life is intense. Parents start the day with great intentions, which can slip away as the day wears on. This is a busy age in which we live, and choosing activities can be tough.

But the pace can change.

"Logistics is a problem when the adult has to be somewhere, such as work, and the child needs to be places too," says a counselor. "Schedules are a big deal. Planning ahead makes a big difference, but there are only so many hours in the day. Learn through trial and error what can wait, what has to be done now, and which approaches work best with your family."

Your Household

Most modern parents use a "timeout" when their children get out of line—that time you make them step back from a

16

situation to regain control. That same approach will work if your family feels frantic.

Give your family a timeout. Discuss ways to ease the schedule.

What must happen to change the pace? Sometimes it is as simple as believing that you have enough time to do what you need to do and that you do not have to hurry. Look for clues as to why your schedule is out of whack. This might be as basic as speaking more slowly and saying no to new activities. It may mean not rushing your children into and out of the car. You may notice certain activities that cause more pressure and need more attention.

"I judge whether or not we have too much on our plates by the level of cheer and composure that we all show," says a Colorado mother of two. "If things start to overheat, we back off a bit."

A big improvement can come by *deciding* to limit your family activities:

- Decide first that you will cut *something* out.
- Next, decide *what* will go.
- Realize that you do not have to cut *everything* out or become like hermits!
- Choose what works for your family and your routine. (Does this sound familiar? You must come back to this idea again and again.)

Discuss with your children what they most like to do, and help them discover and develop their gifts.

"My biggest challenges as a parent involve trying to make the right decisions to help my children become what God wants them to be. I try to encourage the children to try different activities in hopes of finding something that will help them develop a strong sense of self and self-confidence," says a high school teacher and mother of three. As she does that, she works to keep a calm home life. "One thing I do not like is feeling frenzied. Therefore, the children are involved in one to two activities each that usually allow the family to have dinner together at 5:30 and don't keep us out too late."

A preschool teacher and parent adds, "For most of the children I have observed, the schedule of piano one day, soccer another day, and swim team another is just too much."

Choosing Activities

To slow down, get a clear picture of how a less-rushed life might look. Savor that image. Simplify to make it come true. Consider the number of activities your family undertakes and what needs to go.

This requires a fair amount of thought and planning. If you want to keep a relaxed pace, you cannot leave the schedule to chance. You must see how it works for your family. One working father says, "Set priorities, limit activities to one at a time per child, and remember your own childhood memories: what stood out? Think about ways to help your child experience those simple pleasures." A college student who has excelled in academics, athletics, and music stresses the important role her parents played in helping her make hard choices about her schedule through the years: "Parents need to sit their children down and set their priorities straight. They should find out what activities are most important to their children. Once they figure that out, the children should engage in those things. However, if the performance in something slips, such as schoolwork, they have too much on their plate. Life is about balancing, and children will figure out that their bodies can only take on so much."

From her perspective as a college student, this woman feels strongly that children should be involved in activities they enjoy and not be overloaded with a host of things they do not care about: "My mom was always very good at sitting me down and making a schedule that included everything I had to accomplish in a certain amount of time. This helped me tremendously because I came to realize there really was enough time in the day. A schedule would also tell me what I *didn't* have time for. It set my priorities straight. My family was always busy doing something, but for the most part, we made everything work and got everything done."

Level of Involvement

Beyond assisting with activity choices, you must determine how involved you will be. "Your children know whether you are interested in their lives—whether you know who their friends are, whether you are aware of how they are doing in their school and extracurricular activities, and whether you will take the time to be there when they need you," says one father, a retired government executive. He learned from his own parents, something many people say they have done. His father and mother were very involved in his life through the years, from having supper early so he could get to games on time, to coaching his baseball team, "despite having a work situation where asking for time off was a lot harder for my father than it is for me. My dad was good about making time for those teammates whose parents were not able or willing to be around," he says. You truly can touch another person's life when you slow down and become more aware of the needs of others.

Wanting to Give Children Good Things

Sometimes schedules become overloaded for the best of reasons. For example, you want your children and grand-children to have opportunities you missed and to be exposed to interesting parts of life, such as the arts, service to others, or athletics. You want them to learn.

Most parents wrestle with this and give it an astonishing amount of thought. Some have devised time-management systems that work well for their household, and some have tried systems that have failed.

- "We limit the kids to two extracurricular activities—one is mutually agreed upon, such as guitar classes, and the children get to designate their other activity. Usually, church activities are considered apart from this limit," one father said.

- Another family tries this: "We adopted a hard-and-fast rule back when we had only one child, and we have been able to enforce this rule all these years, even now with three kids. The rule is, only one activity or sport per child at any given time. Even still, it takes us as parents a great deal of coordination to maintain full-time work schedules and to make sure the children get to practices, games, and events. If they get overloaded, we have to maintain the balance by redirecting them to what is important. We have always stressed that they need to honor their obligations but not overextend themselves. For example, if they are having trouble getting homework done before activities, we stress that school comes first."

- From a mom in Florida: "I don't have a particular way of deciding which activities the children participate in. I try to let them try anything they want without going crazy. I believe in exposing them to many things in order to help them find what they like to do. Right now our daughter participates in a sport and takes music lessons. One of our sons plays a sport and also has music lessons, and our other son participates in a sport. I have slowed down quite a bit to let them be able to do these events without causing chaos. I am very conscious of not having a chaotic household."

One great challenge is choosing between one good thing and another good thing. Since my first book, *Hurry Less, Worry Less,* I've learned that nearly everyone fights this. If you simply were saying no to bad things, that would be easy. But you also must rule out lots of good things.

"I have always needed a lot of home downtime, so I found myself talking to the girls about moderation," says a woman who stayed home when her children were younger and went back to work as a teacher as they grew. She and her accountant husband stressed to their daughters the importance of priorities: "We were fairly deliberate here. In preschool and elementary school, we allowed one outside activity and one church activity, so as to allow home time and free playtime. As the girls got to middle and high school, we allowed them to set their schedules more and more. We continued to feel strongly that schedules got rapidly out of control without constant monitoring for everyone. As the girls got older, we emphasized adding more service-oriented activities—mission trips, mentoring, food pantries, nursing home visits."

Way Too Busy

Sometimes I bump into people who think it is impossible to slow down. They have set their family life in such fast motion that they cannot see a way to change. This is not an easy mind-set to move beyond, but it can be done.

Think again about the joys of a happy, calm family life, one that is not harried and hectic.

Remember that you make many choices each day. While your work may be tough and your children demanding, you can control much. Do not believe that you are a victim of a schedule that no one can understand but you.

Don't try to live through your children. One teacher says she sees parents pushing their children into too many activities. She asks parents, "Are they doing it because *they* want to do it or because *you* want them to do it?" Overloading children when they are too young can burn them out.

Listen to these words from another parent and ask whether you ever find yourself in a similar situation: "I can become too caught up in my own agenda or hopes for them. After all, how many of us tend to try to live our own lives through our kids? We may never have excelled at anything, and here is this wonderful child who shows early promise in something, and then we get caught up in developing that skill."

Are you pushing your children in areas that are not right for them? Do you want your children to excel for the wrong reasons? Are you caught up in what other people think?

In, Out, Yes, No

Some parents find it hard to say no to their children and add on a class or a team activity even though they suspect it is not right for their child. Then there are the children who want to quit a sport or a class that the parents truly feel is beneficial to them. Some parents invoke the "executive decision" and insist that a child commit to a certain activity. The key here is to communicate why the activity seems important.

Children may beg to do something, such as music lessons or dance classes, and then want to quit. It helps to discuss guidelines in advance. "We discuss what commitment means—follow-through is important, so activities are discussed with the intent of seeing them through. That seems to help in decision making," says a parent with extensive experience in church youth work. "Once you commit, you have to keep this commitment for the amount of time we've paid for and are committed to," adds another.

Activity Overload

When you find your children overwhelmed, help them slow down.

- "Parents need to commit to being in their children's lives. Helping them not get overloaded should be a priority," says a mother of three teens. "If the whole family works together, this can be accomplished. In our family, with three children, making schedules and decisions on school-year activities is all about understanding and compromise. We work together to help each other succeed and become fulfilled."
- Another parent says, "If the children are overloaded because life has just landed that way, I try to help them break down what needs to be done and help them set priorities, and let them know it is OK not to get everything perfect. I also monitor things and try to catch any bad habits and help them get on track."

As with most things in busy families, certain changes must be made through the years. Busy schedules are affected by the size of your family and basic developments, such as whether children are at the same school. You must adjust as life changes, and this may mean that certain seasons stay busy.

Says one mother, "When the older girls were young, we made decisions about activities based on what I thought would be good for them, and that included things both could do at the same time—this meant less driving and better time management. As they got older, and after my husband and I had a third child, the girls developed their own interests, each of which was quite time-consuming, so they could only do one non-school-related activity each, which continues to consume most evenings."

Without a doubt, part of slowing down your family is learning to say no. While *no* is one of the first words we learn as children, it is one of the hardest words to handle as you get older. You agree to do things you do not have time for. You say maybe when your stomach already churns from overdoing it. You keep piling on good causes and worthy activities until you are under the weather and cranky. A sign that it is time to say no is when you hear yourself always talking about how little time you have.

A good verse to use is Matthew 5:37: "Simply let your 'Yes' be 'Yes,' and your 'No,' 'No.' "

A speech therapist working in the school system tells of the importance of adjusting schedules at the beginning of each school year, based on her experience. An overloaded school year with her daughters led to a decision for a more relaxed year. "Organizing the schedule right at the beginning of the school year so that we can have a good, solid, relaxing year has helped immensely," she says. That means comparing schedules, trimming outside activities, and allowing time on weekends to rest and play.

Even with planning and focus, some days will be a mess. "I used to get so worked up if I was not on schedule, but as

I get older, I have started to cherish the experience and enjoy the ride. I may get frustrated, but I try not to let it ruin my entire day," says an executive with two young children.

Talk with your family—your mate, your children, your own parents. Find out what is most important to them. You may be surprised to learn that certain things you are making time for do not matter much.

As you consider where to start, recall what you enjoyed doing as a child, what mattered, what helped you become the person you are. My early family memories include conversations on the front porch, usually involving my parents, who often sat with a cup of coffee in hand; neighbors who were close enough to our family that they wandered in and out of our house; and children gathered with extended family—aunts and uncles, cousins and grandparents—sitting and visiting, often after a great meal. We went to church, belonged to a school club or two, and played a lot. But we did not seem to move all that fast on most days.

My family still puts a premium on sitting and visiting. While it doesn't happen as easily as it did in Mama and Daddy's day, we strive to make it part of our lives.

How about you? What would you like to recapture from your childhood?

Starting Young with a Slower Pace

Children get sucked into busy lives at an early age, with schoolwork and church activities, hobbies, and classes to help them develop interests and skills. They often are so busy *doing* something that they do not have time to *be* children.

Help your children begin from an early age to understand that they do not have to overload and overdo. Life will continue to throw the challenges of busyness at them, so help them learn to make good decisions.

As I was writing this chapter, my nephew e-mailed me a picture of his darling one-year-old daughter. She was sitting in a field of flowers, and my nephew had added a note: "Simple things are best."

Most people who attend my workshops and classes say they want simplicity in their lives. One key way to gain this is to begin to pare down your schedule. Pick and choose, and teach your children to do likewise. Figure out what absolutely cannot be changed, and put everything else on the table for discussion.

And know that tomorrow you will have another chance. "I lie down and sleep; / I wake again, for the LORD sustains me" (Psalm 3:5 NRSV).

Questions to Consider as You Go Forward

- When are you most rushed?
- How do you decide how many activities your family will participate in?
- Do weekly "obligations" need to be trimmed? If so, where and how?

A PRAYER FOR YOUR JOURNEY

Dear Lord, so many things call for our attention. I ask you to help me say no at the right time and to say yes when I should. Watch over my family, especially when they are scattered about, and help them learn how to shape their schedules. Thank you for this day. I praise you for mighty promises and tender mercies; in your holy name. Amen.

Observations from Busy Families

"Kids have better judgment at times than they are given credit for. It's OK to let them fail once in a while in order for them to learn how to get back up and try again."

"One thing I do often now that I have two children is decide what I can reasonably do and what I cannot. I often have to turn down requests in the evenings because that is time set aside for my children. I rarely answer the phone in the evening when I am with my children. We do not leave the television on at our house. We do watch some television, but it is educational and limited."

"There are obviously some things you don't want your child to miss out on. And life gets crazy, especially if you have more than one child. Take a breath and regroup and say no to the next thing. Make sure you don't overcommit, and allow your children to be children."

Quick Tip

"Here's a trick: I keep browned hamburger meat in the freezer for quick meals (spaghetti, chili, and so forth), and I make frozen casseroles over breaks to have something to throw in the oven—*if* I remember to take it out the night before. If someone is trying to establish a pattern of having family meals together, these sorts of timesavers can be a big help."

Chapter Three

THE RHYTHM OF HOME

Encouraging Word: *Your home is a special place.*
Everyday Step: *Sit down and eat a meal together.*

*Even youths grow tired and weary, / and young men
stumble and fall; / but those who hope in
the* LORD */ will renew their strength.*
—Isaiah 40:30-31

*M*y husband and I planted three trees in our yard several
years ago, all the same size, on the same day. One is tall and
flourishes. One looks healthy but grows slowly. The third is
downright scrawny and nearly died. They were all purchased
at the same place and receive the same amount of care.

These trees remind me of families—as different as can be,
even though they have certain things in common. And just
like our trees, families may get different results from the same
efforts. This is particularly true as you think about how you
want to run your household—and it is true as you watch
your children grow as individuals.

When it comes to having a happy home, the formula is
fairly basic: **do more of what works for you.**

When you are on the go most of the time, finding out what works can be a test. To keep a routine in place, you will have to do a course correction from time to time.

Allow time to get up and out the door each morning without frenzy. Set aside time for the chores and duties that flow in at day's end. Have some calm, fun time in the evening. Look for that mix of routine and spontaneity that works for you. Knowing that some things are set in concrete can help you, whether it is the time the children go to bed or the time when you eat supper together. Having other things that you do on the spur of the moment can add zest to life.

As you build your daily routine, put into action a weekly plan, including *who* has to be *where* and *when*. Add time to be home together, including specific meals you will eat as a family. Put time for homework into this plan. Don't forget to allow time for special events, such as birthday parties. And enjoy spontaneity—for example, a friend's family recently spent a school night in a travel trailer parked in their driveway, just for fun.

Having a weekly guide can take you through your schedule with less stress. Be very deliberate in adding *anything* that strains your plan. Keep your tactics in line with your family's needs and wants, and don't try to make them look like those of a friend or neighbor.

Consider this parent's words about family routines, and contemplate what they might mean to your approach: "Budgeting time is as important as budgeting money. I suggest setting aside one evening each week to sit down and go over the next week's schedule. Talk it over together before accepting a big volunteer job. It's great if a family can reserve a night each week or every other week for family fun together. Take turns planning the night. Just slow down—eat together as a family around the kitchen table, talk to each other, read a story or a chapter of a book to your children as you tuck them in bed."

How might you budget your family's time? Can you put "more time together" into each week's plans?

Keeping a happy, fruitful, relaxing, effective routine can be extremely difficult. This is an example of what often happens: The household slips into morning chaos. The children still get up at the same time, but are not getting out the door on time. Their breakfast routine has disappeared. Everyone is tense and rushed and leaves the house angry or near tears.

Step back and realize what is going on. Jot down what needs to happen and when it needs to happen—from getting up to getting dressed to having breakfast to leaving for school. Go over the list with your family, and help them stay on schedule. The result: each member of the family will be calmer, and the days will start better.

This same exercise works with any rough spots in your routine—including homework, bedtime, or making it to church before the benediction.

When you are in a hurry most of the time, it is hard to notice these patterns and to get them under control. This is where allowing even a few minutes of reflection on family life can reward you.

Everyone occasionally slips, but you want frantic mornings to be the exception, not the rule. So it goes for the rest of the day, too, as well as the whole week.

Again, for most people, a happy family life includes a rhythm and routine at home.

This rhythm and routine depends on committing to spending time with your children and allowing time for play. "Children need some unwinding time, just as adults do," says one mother who has been a teacher for thirty years. "They need to be allowed to learn how to entertain themselves with their own things at home, or to read, or to go to the park to meet friends and just play sometimes."

"Time spent with your child is the single biggest asset you have for raising them as you want them to be," says a pediatrician and dad. "A consistent, small amount—an hour here, an hour there—on a regular basis is a good way to connect."

A Routine That Works

Lots of families work hard to establish a routine that works.

- "We have seen that a flexible routine at home provides the children with a comfortable place to be. They know what to expect, but the schedule is not so rigid that changes can't be made in our day or at home. This routine and these consistent expectations help us keep things running smoothly much of the time," says a young mother of two.
- With two teenagers at home, another mom says she helps her children assess how to make things run more smoothly: "I just try to ask questions that might lead them to a solution. I might ask questions such as, 'How important is this to you? What would happen if you didn't go to this event?' Recently, our daughter was staying up really late doing homework. I started asking her why this was the case, and through questioning and making some suggestions, we came up with a goal that she should be done with her homework by 8:45, so that she could begin getting ready to go upstairs and then could get ready for bed and have time to read before turning out the light around 9:30."

- A working mother of two in Tennessee depends on her nightly practices. "We definitely have a routine schedule on school nights. Since my husband works nights, I have to have a strict routine. We do homework at a certain time, baths at a certain time, and bedtime at the same time every night. Supper is cooked at home almost every night."

What's to Eat?

The meal routine is one of the big daily stresses for families, and it can also be one of the times of greatest family joy. Family after family mentions how they aim for meals together, and how that enhances a less-hurried life.

With her children now grown and living on their own, a friend, who is married to a certified public accountant, says, "Make it a priority to eat dinner together. No matter how busy my husband was during tax season, he always came home from the office to eat with the family. I eventually realized it did not have to be a home-cooked meal. We reached a point where just being together was more important than what we ate."

A classmate at church made a similar decision to improve family life: eat less fast food, and have more meals at home. She bemoaned how easy it was to get into the habit of dashing through a drive-through, providing less healthy food, and spending more money. She and her daughters consumed meals on the run, with too little conversation. Like many parents, she is always trying to find ways to make her family life easier and more meaningful. And she makes sure that home is a cozy place where the family can have fun and relax. Concerns about eating out were woven through all of that.

Eating out too often started out of "total convenience," she says. "We're hungry and on the other side of town from home, so, 'Oh, here, let's eat out.'" Now she plans meals on the weekend and comes up with a weekly menu, an idea she got from a friend. "It is so much easier," she says. She has the ingredients at home along with a plan for what they will eat. "Eating out has become our treat instead of our habit."

Have you found yourself in a similar pattern, turning in to a drive-through too often, eating in a hurry in the car, having a meal where you do not talk with your children? How can you alter those habits?

Another family offers this perspective: "We decided that whenever possible, we would eat at the kitchen table as a family, just engaging with one another. This has gotten increasingly difficult with a greater number of activities. But every time all five of us are home, or at least the majority of us, we have dinner at the table."

"We have meals together as a family, and that's very important," says the mother of three. "We don't eat out much because it never seems like we're really there together, and because I have trouble hearing in a crowded restaurant, there are so many distractions."

Sit down at the table where you would like to enjoy meals with your children. Picture it. Grab a notebook and make a list of steps to make it happen—patterns you will change and new approaches you'll take. Consider easy food that you can have at home.

"Don't hold yourself to the standards of other families," says one parent. "Do what works for your family. That goes for chores, allowances, activities, meals. I know lots of families eat breakfast together, but that did not work for our family. The kids were not good at getting up in the morning, and I would get mad because they did not have time to eat the breakfast I fixed for them. I quit fixing breakfast, let them get something out of the pantry, and we all were happier."

Look for ways to make mealtime happy and memorable in your home.

Seasons of Time

Your family will change as the years pass, and old ideas may not work anymore. Your babies become teens, who become adults. Your parents age and need your care in new ways, requiring a different approach to your time with them. Your siblings scatter, and those relationships require added attention. Within your family, you will go through many seasons of time, and you will need flexibility to deal with all those changes. This process of change starts early, and you might as well get used to it.

A father, after the birth of his first child, speaks of the adjustments that started immediately: "I don't think we've arrived anywhere on time yet. Almost everything revolves around my son's feeding schedule or sleeping schedule. Even if that works just right, it takes an extra thirty minutes to get ready to leave the house with the baby. You just have to be patient and realize that it rarely matters if you're a little late for something. I used to be so embarrassed about not getting to church on time that I almost wouldn't go if we were going to be five minutes late. Now, if we get there sometime between 9:00 A.M. and noon, I think we did pretty good."

Have you ever found yourself in a similar position?

Enjoy each season of time, and don't fret about the little things.

Focus on the season of time. Many decisions about your daily life will depend on the ages of your children. Recognizing this can keep you from trying to do too much. When a child is an infant and needs constant care, you find yourself with scarcely a moment to spare. As the kids get older, they can dress themselves and do their own homework and become more independent—then, they need your guidance but not your constant oversight.

Keep these seasons in mind with friends and relatives too. Be sensitive to times they need someone to step in and help. This can be a good way for siblings or grandparents to make a difference. "Offering to babysit or to host an overnight visit is a great thing for everyone," says a grandmother of two and a veteran child-care provider. "Suggesting that the parents have a date night can create quality time for you with your grandchild and can be a big help to the parents."

When Things Seem Out of Control

Even if you generally do a great job with everyday life, you can find yourself swamped at times. Going back to school, wrapping up the end of the school year, holidays—there are often times when you have more to do than you can calmly handle. Those special times require good plans and patience because they can upset your family's routine.

To deal with such times, be ready for them. If you expect a slower pace all of the time, you will be dismayed. Not only will you have added activities on your calendar, but you will have more stress in your life.

Each family has its own busy times of year, but certain things are constant.

Back to School

- Begin to shift gears as the school year approaches. Help your children get back into their school routine, including getting to bed at the right time and getting up earlier if needed.
- Help them enjoy this time of year, a time for a fresh start, seeing old friends, meeting new people, and moving along in school. You can mold their attitude about school in the ways you talk about it with them and in the relaxed way you handle it. If you complain and are in a frenzy, they will pick up on that.
- Make a list of what you have to do each fall, and work your way through it in advance. Don't put off until the last minute buying school supplies or getting cash for school fees.
- Consider asking a younger child to decorate a fun box to put lists and supplies in, which can help to keep him or her organized and get him or her involved in part of the process.

Sometimes children are anxious about returning to school. They have enjoyed their time off and may not know their new teacher or their classmates. My mother always went back to the Golden Rule at this time of year: "Do to others as you would have them do to you" (Luke 6:31). She paraphrased it in her Mom words: "You be nice to them, and they'll be nice to you."

The Hectic Days of Christmastime

At about Thanksgiving, the world speeds up. Parents tell me again and again how difficult this time of year is. The second book in the "Hurry Less, Worry Less" series, *Hurry Less, Worry Less at Christmastime,* was born of the frustration so many encounter in trying to rejoice and enjoy that sacred time of year. While everyday life is pretty tough for many, the Christmas season piles on levels of challenges in both hurry and worry. Families schedule too much and battle trying to get different family members together, which often includes helping children and stepchildren arrive at the right place at the right time. No matter how much money parents make, they feel that the holidays cost too much. They worry about overspending, overeating, and generally overdoing.

- Decide early to approach the holiday season differently. Before Thanksgiving, take a few minutes to list activities you want to do more of through Christmas, and things you want to do less of.
- Draw up a budget and stick to it, no matter how difficult it is. Do not spend more than you can afford.
- Attend worship with your family, and enjoy the season of Advent, those weeks of anticipation and celebration of the birth of Christ.
- Put family time on your calendar, and let your children decide what you will do. Maybe they'll want to watch a family Christmas movie and make cookies. Perhaps they like to look at Christmas lights in the neighborhood or drink hot chocolate and decorate the tree.

Christmastime is a holy, special time for families. It can be fun and fulfilling—but you will need to step back and identify personal ways to slow it down. You especially might focus on the week after Christmas, a time when things sometimes slow down a bit. This takes planning, but it can bring sweet rewards.

"We had a nice Christmas break this year because we were more intentional about slowing down and doing less," one father says. "We did not try to do everything packed into a small amount of time. We did not travel or overcommit. We enjoyed each other, played laser tag, and slowed down."

The memories you provide will be vibrant. You'll be glad you made needed changes.

Springtime Activities

During the weeks just before summertime, things go surprisingly fast. Picture a child on a skateboard, well under control, picking up speed. Then more speed, with less control.

So goes this time of year. And somehow it seems to catch families off guard.

Students have recitals, special programs at church, and end-of-school parties. Families celebrate graduations—from kindergarten and middle school to high school and college. Many weddings are planned for spring and early summer, drawing family members into wedding showers and dinners and ceremonies. Mother's Day, a special day for families to say thank you for Mom's love and care, comes along. Mix in Easter and spring break, and *voilà*! You wonder *again* if you can possibly slow your family down.

- Once more, plan in advance. Put dance recitals, concerts, out-of-town trips, and family occasions on your calendar.
- Take a hard look at what you are trying to do. What plans can you eliminate? Perhaps you want to attend a high school baccalaureate, but it clashes with a spring choir concert. Trim some things from your schedule; you cannot do it all.

- Mix events that feel like obligations with activities that you and your family enjoy.
- Return as needed to your family's rhythm and routine, eating together, touching base in the evenings, making mornings calmer, whatever works best for you.
- Do not overspend on outfits, gifts, and extras. This is another time of year when money can pour out of your wallet. Keep the family budget in mind. You will feel better if you do not overspend.

A Slower Season

When I was a child, summer was a slow season, a time for playing outdoors until it was so dark you could not see anything. We waited, sweaty and worn out, for our mothers to call us in for the night.

The flow of summertime has changed, but it can still be a time to play and connect in relaxed ways, a time to slow down and have fun together.

"When the children were younger, we would book nothing for summers," says one mom. "They had their summers off. No piano lessons or planned activities, with the exception of a church camp or football camp. We kept life simple. They worked hard all year and did quite well. This was their time to watch movies, play outside, read books, paint, have friends over, and all the fun summer things that we do. Upon entering high school, they now have mandatory football practices and cheer camps, but otherwise, we still keep it simple."

Plan time off from work while your children are out of school. Perhaps vacation time off from work is hard to come by, and you can only take off a day or two. If so, take a long weekend and do something together as a family.

Play. Spend more time outside. Enjoy the long daylight hours, when it stays light outside until close to bedtime.

Have a picnic in your yard or at a nearby park. Don't feel the need to make it fancy. Just make it fun. As one grandmother says, "Picnics in the backyard are a big hit. And, boy, they'll eat anything in that setting!"

Attend vacation Bible school. This is a fun way to connect children with church and to help them learn Bible stories. Many churches have VBS in the evenings now and also offer classes for parents. Use this as a family fun time and as a time to build the spiritual component of your life.

Go to the library. Summertime is the perfect time for building a love of reading, a goal many parents have for their children. Get a library card for your child and have fun picking out books together. Many public libraries have great summertime programs for children, including free activities that are entertaining and educational. One friend regularly shares with her grandkids "the treasures of the public library," as she calls them, pointing out the availability of books, movies, magazines, and more—all for free. "We are so privileged to have these resources," she says.

Get out of your rut. Be creative. One family always celebrated the longest day of the year with dessert for supper. Another family has elderly friends over for hot dogs on the Fourth of July. Look for ways to enjoy summer more.

These seasons remind us of the ebb and flow of life. "For everything there is a season, and a time for every matter under heaven," says Ecclesiastes 3:1 (NRSV). While you know that life will be busy, look for ways to have a rhythm that meets the needs of your family.

One single young adult says this about family plans: "Family time is a time when problems are solved and everyone can repair from the day. Life is too short to be hurrying and worrying all of the time. However, we do live in the twenty-first century. Hurrying is going to happen every once in a while because the pace of the world around us is speeding up. Families should try to do as much as they can and still be 'sane' people. Life is also about experiencing many different things, and children and adults should make the most out of their lives. Yet life is about balancing, and families should set limits. If that means activities have to be given up, then that is what needs to happen."

I wince when I think of hurrying my young granddaughter, who moves at such a delightful pace. She does not hurry. What I have learned from her is that I must do a better job at setting our schedule, allowing time to get ready, and getting out the door and where we need to be. That lessens our stress immensely, and we enjoy outings so much more. Learn from your children.

Questions to Consider as You Go Forward

- What does having a happy home mean to you?
- How might you make mealtimes more enjoyable for your family?
- What is the busiest season for your children or grandchildren, and what are some ideas for helping them more fully enjoy this season?

A PRAYER FOR YOUR JOURNEY

Dear God, thank you for our home. Please surround it with your love and care. Keep it safe, and make it a place of kindness and joy. May it be a place of encouragement and acceptance. Help me teach my family in ways that will make them strong and loving; in the precious name of Christ. Amen.

Observations from Busy Families

"Certain times of the year, depending on my work schedule and the holidays, we hurry more than usual. But we always try to spend downtime or family time with just the three of us together. You can get very caught up all the time in being somewhere where others want you to be, but we make a conscious effort not to stretch ourselves, or our young daughter, too thin."

"Make your home a sanctuary—a place where your children feel safe and loved and secure."

"Do simple things with your family. Play together; eat together at home."

Quick Tip

"The best rule—we had odd and even days for who got to sit in the front seat. That cut out all fights over who sat in the front every time we got into the car."

Chapter Four

ORGANIZE TO ENERGIZE

Encouraging Word: *You can clear out clutter at home.*
Everyday Step: *Throw something away.*

Look to the LORD and his strength;
seek his face always.
—1 Chronicles 16:11

*T*he quest for household organization takes on mythical status with most busy families. The search for a clean kitchen counter and an uncluttered family room is like the search for the Holy Grail.

Because mail, school papers, folders, and miscellaneous stuff keeps coming in, the problem is never exactly fixed. Add in laundry waiting to be washed or folded, and you can almost hear your blood pressure rising.

Parents frequently list "getting organized" as one of the things they would do if they had time. For many, it would even be fun—to go through the house with a trash bag and a sword, cutting a path through chaos and regaining control of their kingdom.

"What do you do with all that stuff that comes out of your kids' backpacks?" asks one mother. "My daughter had a pinecone today, which was so sweet . . . before it was stepped on. And school sends so much paperwork home."

Having a comfortable home, one that is calm and restful, is a goal of many parents and grandparents. It is certainly one of mine.

As you consider what you want your family life to be like, give thought to how you live in your home. For many people, this includes eating meals together as a family. It includes time to visit and play together. It includes being organized enough to know where to find important papers without having to tear the place apart.

Thinking about Home

Your home's personality says a lot about your family's attitude.

Does it give you a good feeling when you walk in the door? Is it comfortable? Are there good areas for family interaction, whether in a den or the breakfast nook? Do you come together as a family, or all move in separate orbits? Notice homes in which you are comfortable, and consider why they make you feel that way.

When I was growing up, our house was an old rental, slightly on the shabby side. Our family of six shared one bathroom, and we had window unit air conditioners and space heaters. But people congregated at our home. When I had a home of my own, I realized my mother's gift of making people feel welcome. When someone popped in at mealtime, my mother shared our food. She encouraged friends whose home lives were rough. She was kind and generous.

Some people are more formal by nature. They may want their home to be bare, without piles of books and magazines. Others (like my husband and me) are borderline pack rats, with a fair amount of clutter and a house where you can put your feet up on the coffee table. We like books, magazines, music, DVDs, and antiques. Mix those, and you have a lot of stuff to dust. We must constantly step back and de-clutter, or our comfortable nest resembles a junk shop.

Look for details to make your home special. For example, a teacher has two large maps tacked to her breakfast room wall—one map of the United States and one map of the world. "We put pushpins in the U.S. map on places we have been," she says. "When friends adopted a daughter from the Democratic Republic of the Congo, we found it on the map. When Rotary Club members from Turkey were visiting friends of ours, the children were able to find it on the map. It helps the children understand their place in the world, helps them understand directions, and aids in learning geography."

We have adopted this idea. When we plan a family vacation, my husband puts a map on the kitchen wall, marking our route. It not only teaches us about where we are going, it adds to the anticipation of the trip. Our granddaughter has a globe at our house, so Papa can show her where Mexico is or how Europe looks, and so she can just have fun identifying faraway places.

Homes are made special with simple touches. One of my sisters-in-law keeps a basket of old toys—long outgrown by her sons—for visiting children. Another has kept her grown daughter's dollhouse, a favorite for every little girl who comes over.

A Special Place

Home can be one of those spectacularly warm places, the spot where you open the door and are transported away from the world. Perhaps you know the feeling of walking into your childhood home and knowing the smell and a certain feeling in an instant.

To create the kind of home you want does not take a lot of money. You might *like* to throw out the torn recliner and replace the worn carpet with hardwood floors, but you do not have to go that far.

Take time to think about the kind of home you want. Walk through each doorway with new eyes. Consider what needs to be tossed and what might be moved around. Once more, yield to the season of time you are in. Maybe you have a refrigerator door covered with original artwork from a preschooler. Perhaps you have a line of framed school pictures in the hall or a basket of vacation pictures on the hearth. Your coffee table may be covered with toys or juice cups or rocks picked up at the park.

Chat with your family, perhaps at supper one night, about what they want the house to look like. Even by age seven, our granddaughter had strong opinions about colors and decor. It is fun to look through a decorating or home magazine with her, seeing what rooms she likes and why. When I built my office, I asked for her opinion, and I was amazed at the creative thoughts she had.

Cooperation

Comfortable homes need some degree of tidiness—and that doesn't just *happen*. Most families try to spread the work routine around, sharing duties. "Delegate," says one dad.

Teach your children about helping out in the world by guiding them to help at home. This is a way, too, to help them discover their gifts. Most children can help in the kitchen, no matter how young they are. They can set the table and put out napkins. Give them small jobs to keep them involved and to help them feel useful.

As they get older, some children like to cook. Build on this to help them develop a skill that will be meaningful for many years. Let younger children help you in simple ways.

Don't forget yard work, even if it means just picking up stray sticks or sweeping the driveway. Older children can help rake and mow. My niece and I like to go on a "litter patrol" when we are at the lake, putting on work gloves and filling a large trash sack. The neighborhood looks better as a result, and we have a sense of accomplishment.

"If I was starting fresh, I would have established independence in my children from the beginning," says one mom. "My sister has four boys, ages twelve, eight, three, and one. The two older ones each have responsibilities—the eight-year-old cleans up after dinner, and the twelve-year-old gives the three-year-old a bath. They both bathe themselves and do homework themselves. My sister taught each of her sons from as early an age as possible to do things for themselves, and now they do."

Organized at Home

Being organized adds to the quality of life in a variety of ways. It can end the frantic search for a piece of paper that needs to go back to school immediately. It can help your children learn how to keep track of everything from toys to money.

One young mom depends on household organization to keep her on track: "I like to plan things in advance as often as possible, and I try to keep my house in pretty good order, which means cleaning on the weekends. I don't feel in control unless my house is relatively clean. Bills are paid online, and usually on Fridays. I keep calendars both on the wall and in my purse to keep up with appointments. I keep files on all important matters. The kids help with major projects around the house, and my husband helps take care of the house and does all of the yard work. Sometimes I keep sticky notes on my purse and on my wallet to remind me of errands I need to run."

Do you have a system—or need one? What small step might you take to get more organized at home?

Use a List

In my experience, nothing works better than a list. Instead of becoming overwhelmed by all that you have to do, enjoy marking off what you have accomplished. Write each task down so you won't forget it, whether it's scheduling an orthodontist appointment for your youngest child or picking up the dry cleaning.

"I try hard to stay organized with a list of things that need to be managed both at home and at work," says a mother of two small children. "Of course, this is often a very long list for both. I try to look at what I can reasonably get done and get something accomplished each day. I do my best not to let the little things pile up."

Organizing Homework

Having a system for organization helps. This is particularly true in dealing with homework, a topic that agitates many parents and students. "Success for a child in school is like a triangle, with the teacher, the student, and the parent being at each point," says a parent and teacher. "It takes all three for children to be most successful and reach their full potential."

Another mom agrees: "I am very involved with my children's education. You learn a lot about a school when you become involved. My volunteer work helped me build relationships with teachers and administrators, and also with other parents. My children know that education is important to our family. I value the schools, the teachers, and the administrators."

"We try to keep a super-structured schedule," says one mother. "The child's homework is started as soon as we get home. It is usually finished before supper. We try to keep our daughter's desk, her homework area, extremely organized, so we don't forget on Thursday homework that was sent home on Monday. At our house, we have a homework clipboard. On the clipboard we keep the assignments sent home at the beginning of the week that aren't due until a later date, and every night we check the board. It's not great, but it's the best system we have come up with so far."

The Children's Room

A closely related topic that leads to the frequent need for a family ceasefire is that of children's rooms, and their state of disarray. Parents find themselves torn between cleaning up the room themselves and trying to wait out their children, while the laundry piles up.

Some parents declare they will not go into their child's room until it is picked up, and that clothes must be delivered to the laundry room if they are to be washed. That usually lasts a few days, until Mom or Dad cannot stand it anymore. They angrily retrieve the dirty clothes, straighten the messy room, and snap at their children. More than one fun family weekend has been ruined by this clash.

Most people crave organization and are always seeking ways to cut down on clutter. Teaching children to help around the house is an ongoing cause of stress but a way that many parents find helps their family life be less hurried and worried. Here is how one family handles chores: The parents and their two children have a regular list of chores for which they use both games and rules to manage. They require chores to be done before weekend fun begins—including activities such as computer games or visits from friends—with a clear message that doing your part without complaint is part of life. As the father says, "The thing that bugs us most (although we shouldn't let it) is that many other kids their age don't have chores. This is a family. Everyone can contribute to varying degrees. If we aren't working together on this thing, then parents are just caretakers. Everyone can do something. Early on, kids want to help. It's our job to make sure they don't lose that desire to cook, clean, and be a full partner at home."

Could you make cleaning-time part of your evening routine, while having some fun doing it? Might your children, whatever their ages, have a part in this? The family above, for example, sets a timer and works to see what each person can get done in a certain amount of time.

Feedback from different parents shows that you might want to start at an early age with chores, and make it a part of everyone's home life. "If I had it to do over, I would start off earlier having them clean up after themselves. I don't have very neat children, and I think this is from my not being consistent with them in this area. It would make day-to-day living much easier for our whole family if we all picked up after ourselves and had more chores to do on a regular basis," says one mother.

Helping your child learn to keep a tidy, if not spotless, room is a great gift—one for which your children's college roommates, or their future spouses, or both, will one day thank you. If this causes constant friction in your family, sit down together and talk about possible solutions. You may have to give up on your dream of being the cover story for a home decorating magazine, but perhaps your child will better understand where you are coming from. And perhaps keeping a clean room is one of those requirements for having other privileges.

"We try to foster independence by having the kids do chores (honestly, not a ton of chores, but a handful each week), keep track of their own homework, make their own lunches, set up their own social plans, and so forth," says one mother of teens.

The World of Technology

When I was in the eighth grade, a friend's parents would not let her watch *Perry Mason* on television after school. I was allowed to watch, which caused some consternation. While that courtroom drama is not high on family discussion lists these days, the topics of television and other technology continue to be a challenge for parents.

"I see TV and video games getting in the way," says an elementary schoolteacher in Texas. "So many kids now stay indoors and don't play outside. Kids, even at a young age, have TVs in their bedrooms. This interferes with sleep and with communication in the family, and parents may be unaware of what their kids are watching." An overuse of television, computers, and cell phones affects children's schedules and their use of time for other endeavors.

Another teacher adds, "Good, quality television and movies are not bad in and of themselves—it's just that watching them too much is such a passive activity. It does not stimulate much creativity, nor does it help children interact with others. It's great in small doses; watch with your children and discuss what you saw. Hit the pause button occasionally and ask them how they think the story will end or what they would do if they were the main character. Research shows that these types of questioning activities encourage children to read and write more."

You must decide what you will allow your family to watch on television or view on the computer, and how much time you will permit for those activities.

"I used to have a one-hour rule," says a parent. "They could be on the computer or watch TV for one hour a day, total. But they really don't spend a lot of time with either activity now. If they get a new game, I let them play it as much as they want for a few days or a week, and then I start limiting it again. When they were a little younger, I had them not use any technology for a week if they seemed to be getting addicted. I would tell them that they were not being punished or in trouble, but that we needed to break the habit."

For one family, another approach works better: "A major decision we've made is that we don't have cable television. In today's age, this is very odd, I know, but I do think it has really changed the chemistry of our family."

Consider television carefully. Listen to these mothers' words and see if you agree or disagree:

"If I could do it again, I never would have started my children out watching television at all—no matter how cute and educational the shows may seem or how easy it was to put them in front of the TV so that I could get things done," says one mother. "Even the shows made for the family and for children are getting to be difficult to monitor and are providing terrible role models."

"I think the biggest waste of time for families today is watching television," says another mother. "I can't imagine that many kids are going to remember that fondly as a family activity. I hear adults talk about the different shows they watch regularly, and it blows my mind that this is how they choose to spend their time. Well, there's my 'soapbox'!"

You must find what is right for you. For some families, it might be no television. For others, it might be an hour a night or a certain program each week. Make your choices deliberately, and consider the outcome you want for your children.

The Challenge of the Computer

Another test for families these days is the use of the computer—a great educational tool, a fun toy, and also a potential hazard. Many parents put the computer in an area of the house within full view, for regular checks on their children's viewing. Other families share computer time, with restrictions on what can be accessed.

While writing this book, I've heard more than one horror story about teens getting online and being preyed upon by adults. Parents who are involved in their children's lives can help prevent this.

Time on the Computer

The Internet puts the world at your child's fingertips and, therefore, requires a close eye. You want to keep your children safe from those who use the Web as a weapon and help your children understand what is not appropriate.

Set up rules, and help children understand what you expect. When we have young relatives as overnight guests, we allow them to mix computer use with other games and activities, but their use is limited.

Decide where the computer will be placed in your home. Many parents prefer to have their computers in open areas where they can keep an eye on what children see online.

Have rules for permissible Web sites.

For example, one single mom allows her young daughters to use only Web sites she has listed as "favorites." They can play on these certain sites but can give no personal information or sign up for anything.

Resist the urge to "park" children at the computer or the television for long periods of time, and don't forget other technological temptations.

The Internet is not the only type of technology that demands attention. Consider the cell phone, which typically includes text messaging and camera options. Each family must decide when it is OK for a child to have a phone, or if one is needed at all, and what the rules for the phone's use will be. Some families like for their children to be accessible by phone at all times. Others try to keep phone use to a minimum.

While you are at it, take stock of your own time on the phone, and whether that too often takes you away from conversations with your children.

Talk with your children about their use of phones, including the camera and access to the Internet. Make the rules clear, and stick by them. Keep a watchful eye, and be alert for potential problems, especially in communication that may not be appropriate for children their age.

Cell phones and playtime on the computer can be used to reward good behavior or as part of overall activities. One woman, for example, allowed her daughter to have text messaging after she consistently made good grades. The messaging is a reward, but it requires her keeping her grades up.

"Our computer is located centrally in the house where I can monitor the use," says the mom of three. "My husband suggested purchasing one for the girls' room, but I said no. I want to be able to monitor them, and I cannot do this behind a closed door. I do not set a time limit for the computer's use, but with it being located in the open, I can easily tell if they have been sitting at it too long. I can view the screen to see if they are doing research or surfing."

Handling the Little Things

If you are a busy parent, you know a secret: the big issues are not always the ones that worry you. Often the little things become nagging problems and weigh parents down—for example, the last-minute dash to the store to pick up a gift for a birthday party or the scramble to find a clean pair of socks before baseball practice.

Devise your own efficient systems for these problems and tasks. Think back on what has worked, and what caused stress. Don't turn these little issues into big deals.

Figure out how you will deal with birthday party invitations—transportation; providing activities for other children, if that is an issue; and what you will do for gifts, including how much to spend.

"I discovered this year that a wonderful way to deal with all the birthday parties is to have a standard gift on hand—two or three, actually, and then I don't have to shop in a rush. That's made a big difference," says one parent.

You may have to turn down some party invitations, even some from people you care about, says another mother. "With three daughters, we can get bogged down in birthday party invitations. Sometimes we make it to the party; sometimes we send a present and call it a day. We have learned that we can't please everyone, so we just draw our boundaries when we feel overwhelmed."

These words from another parent describe a sentiment shared by many parents: "The hardest thing for me is keeping all the schedules straight and making the connections. 'Friday night out' doesn't just mean Friday night out. It means hiring a babysitter, providing an easy meal for the sitter and the kids, and so on. 'A birthday party' doesn't just mean a birthday party. It means finding a gift and figuring out how to manage the other two kids in terms of where they need to go. I know that sounds really weird, like, 'How dumb do you have to be?'; but I mess that up all the time."

Set up schedules. Learn to deal with nagging problems. Let some things go. Throw away stuff on a regular basis, or donate it to be used by someone who really needs it. Clearing clutter can help clear your brain. Your home is where you will change lives.

Questions to Consider as You Go Forward

- What annoys you most about your daily household organization?
- What three steps can you take to cut back on clutter?
- What is one thing you would most like your family's help with?

A PRAYER FOR YOUR JOURNEY

Dear Lord, help me stay focused on what is truly important. Give me strength to tackle household duties with energy and love. Help me guide my family, and help us grow together as a team and assist one another without complaint; in your holy name. Amen.

Observations from Busy Families

"We always review our day and figure out what we could do to make it better. On weekends, we try to do one fun thing together. That can be as simple as going out for ice cream or dinner."

"Be there for the important stuff, the events for each family member. Much of the time this comes at the expense of having a clean house, because the more important thing is getting to the game or helping with homeroom."

"Stay focused on what's important. If you have to put in more hours at the office, learn to work more efficiently so that you can get out on time to have dinner with your family. Make sure you make it a priority to go to your son's football game or your daughter's soccer practice. There may be times when you have to miss a game or two, but try to limit that."

Quick Tip

"Pick your battles. Don't argue about the little things."

Chapter Five

A FOUNDATION
OF FAITH

Encouraging Word: *Your family can build*
a deep spiritual life.
Everyday Step: *Say a prayer together.*

"If anyone is thirsty, let him come to me and drink.
Whoever believes in me, as the Scripture has said, streams
of living water will flow from within him."
—John 7:37-38

The idea of sleeping in on Sundays can be mighty enticing. Getting the family up, dressed, and out the door to church on time can be nerve-racking for lots of families. And that stress doesn't even include worrying about breakfast! But setting the alarm clock to get up in time for church is often the big leap families take to move forward spiritually, and to make deep changes in how they live.

Maybe your desire to build a faithful family started younger, with your own spiritual journey. Or maybe you have gotten so busy that you let slip your habit of praying and attending church. As you look for ways to slow your family down and to worry less, get your spiritual motor running. You need this for the strength to get through the busy days at home and at work. You need it to help you be the kind of parent you want to be. And you need it to help your children build a faithful foundation that will guide them through life. This *really* matters.

In today's jumbled, stressed-out world, imparting a faith in God to your family can be a calming, joyful experience. It's sort of like watching a snow globe settle down after you've given it a good, hard shake. A strong faith and commitment to God's guidance can make a tremendous difference for your family. As you teach about God's love and the gift of Jesus Christ, you help your children learn about loving others and being kind and generous. You help them become servants at a young age, as well as thoughtful persons who notice others who are hurt or sad or in need.

As God's love infuses your life, you can develop a spirit of gratitude for what is going right and less worry for what might be going wrong.

Stop again to consider your priorities.

- What do you want your children to know and believe?
- What do you want to expose them to?
- How do biblical teachings fit in?

For most, this issue involves struggles, questions, and the need to regroup and recommit—again and again. A commitment to faith, worship, and church activities usually does not just happen. It is planned and intentional. It overcomes the urge to sleep in or to do one of dozens of other things on a Sunday morning. It even transcends grumpy kids who think they would rather stay home and sleep or play.

Think about your own family as you read how this parent handled the issue of church: "Our first decision as we began to have children was to get back into church. Like so many younger people, we had drifted from the daily routines, but we knew we wanted our children to grow up in church. I've always wanted them to *want* to go, not feel *made* to go. Somehow it has worked for us."

A Relationship with God

Perhaps you are uneasy discussing this topic, or you feel that you do not know enough about the Bible or how to pray. You may have made a variety of mistakes and have regrets; most of us do.

Consider your own faith. Maybe you haven't attended church in years and need to start. Or perhaps you've been an occasional churchgoer but have never gone beneath the surface of worshiping. Think about attending a Sunday school class or having a conversation with a pastor.

"Look to the LORD and his strength; seek his face always" (1 Chronicles 16:11). You will find your parenting duties to be much easier when you follow those words.

Turn to God in prayer for your own spiritual journey and for that of your family. Pray for wisdom and patience. If you are uncomfortable praying, just ask God for help. "Help, Lord. Help me. Help my family."

This spiritual dimension sometimes leaves parents feeling as though they have fallen short; that they have erred; that they have not been faithful. Thankfully, our God is a God of second—and third and fourth—chances.

Allow yourself quiet time—even when it is difficult. Be still and let the cares of the day roll away. Read the Bible and find verses that encourage you as a parent.

One mother mentions Psalm 139 as a comfort. That passage includes these words: "O Lord, you have searched me / and you know me. / You know when I sit and when I rise; / you perceive my thoughts from afar. / . . . For you created my inmost being; / you knit me together in my mother's womb. / I praise you because I am fearfully and wonderfully made; / your works are wonderful, I know that full well" (Psalm 139:1-2, 13-14).

"This passage reminds me that God is active in parenting, even from inside the womb," says that mother. "It helps me feel that God is with me in everything I do at work, at home, and at play. This Scripture reminds me that I am not alone as a parent, but that God—who knows me inside out and who helped form me in my mother's womb—also guides my thoughts and lifts me up every day. This passage also reminds me that God is active in my son's life and created him in God's own image."

A Family Matter

Sometimes your spouse or your children may not want to go to church. Try to communicate your feelings about this and why it is important for your family. In conversations such as these, remember James 1:19: "Everyone should be quick to listen, slow to speak and slow to become angry." This verse is a fine one to remember, by the way, in all difficult family discussions.

Perhaps you have gone to church without your spouse, unsure whether to go alone or stay home. Or maybe you've cajoled your partner with no success. Says one mom: "I started going to church by myself and becoming involved with activities there. As time went on and my husband could see that it was important to me, and how I changed for the better, he started joining me at church. And the children have followed suit. We have a great youth group, so that helps a lot to fill in what we may lack in communicating our beliefs. I try to live by the principles of the Bible at home and not contradict what we all learn in church."

Pray with your children. Teach them to say thank-you for food at mealtimes and to go to God in prayer before they go to sleep. Help them learn to pray for others and to consider those who are sick or facing problems. You can guide them at a young age to be aware of the needs of others.

Read Bible stories together. When children are young, choose picture books and discuss the stories. As they get older, read together from the Bible. Consider together how these lessons apply to their everyday lives and the situations they may face, whether they are elementary school students who are hurt when they are left out of a game or teens wrestling with their future.

Weave discussions of faith and trust in God into your daily life. "Our faith is a very important choice that shapes our family life," one parent said to me. "We want our child to grow up aware that we are dependent on God, who created us, sustains us, and continues to love us all, even when we mess up. It is important to us that we model God's love to one another in our family and that we show God's love to others in the world who might be different from us. We use mealtimes and bedtimes to offer prayers to God; we read stories from the Bible together; and we try to encourage our son to give back to others and to love others."

A Church Family

In today's busy world, attending church can be easy to take off the to-do list. A mother of three children stresses that you have to move church up on your list of priorities. "You have to go, and you have to go regularly, or it never becomes a habit and you won't go. We're all given the exact same number of minutes in our week. So it's all a matter of priorities and how we spend those minutes."

She is blessed by her church involvement: "I love the environment of church. I love the people and what I do when I'm there. I need church every week in order to reconnect and 'reset.' I think that feeling spreads to the kids, and we try to let them participate in any extra church-related activities they want to do."

A Louisiana attorney with two college-age daughters and a recently adopted seven-year-old says that he and his wife decided early on that church was a priority. "We gave up sleeping in on Sunday, which also required that we go to bed at a reasonable time on Saturday night. Communicating this to the girls was easy. They were young and had no real choice in the beginning. We then tried to be in tune to their needs. We found a church that spoke in relevant language they could understand and, more important, apply. We prayed together as a family and sought God's guidance for our lives. We encouraged the children to pray out loud with us. We admitted our faults to one another and made amends to one another. Most of all, we taught grace and mercy for others by example, and not just by words."

At the church I attend, we sing a wonderful song when someone is baptized, to welcome the person into our church family. The song reminds me that church can be an intimate part of each person's life, starting with childhood. We are bound together at church, and we help one another grapple with hard questions and celebrate life's victories. Through church, parents can find support for the challenges of ordinary life and extraordinary developments.

Participate as a family in worship. Sing. Listen. Attend worship regularly, not just at Christmas and Easter.

Find classes and small-group activities that work for you and for your children. Commit to these. By going beyond worship, you can grow in spiritual maturity and be better equipped to teach your children. They, on the other hand, will embark on their own journey and become comfortable talking about faith, asking questions, and enjoying church. And you will get to know dear people at a much deeper level.

Depend upon your church family to help you with your family. This mother sums it up clearly: "Kids are faced with so many opportunities to make poor choices, and sometimes parents just aren't enough. I think we need help from others who also care about the paths our children will take, and who will help teach them about the choices they make and the consequences of those choices, and reinforce what we are trying to teach. Sometimes things are taken differently coming from those who don't spend all their time parenting and disciplining and correcting and loving because they have to. Fitting church in isn't always easy, but it is a priority in our house."

When Children Don't Want to Go to Church

Many of us have been through times when we neglected church. Perhaps we were testing our wings in high school or college or when starting out as a young professional, or perhaps we just were not interested for some reason. But family worries can expand when children do not want to go to church. Many families let their children know it is not optional and gently but firmly make it happen.

A young friend who attended church from her preschool days tells this story, a nice reassurance to parents who are struggling with the weekly war: "An issue I see again and again is that families are not telling their children about the importance of faith in their lives. As a result, the kids decide to leave the church because they don't think church is the 'cool' thing to do. Parents need to teach their children it is OK to be different from their friends. It is important to learn about Christ. The more children are in church and learning about the Bible, the more they will respect and love their parents. I know this is true for my friends and me. There was a time when I literally was forced to go to Sunday school and youth group. I really don't remember why this was the case, other than the fact that I was just of that age when I didn't understand the importance of faith. Nonetheless, my parents continued to push my faith, and I am forever grateful to them for that."

A college student from the Houston area agrees: "Church has meant everything to me growing up. I rarely missed a Sunday because I loved going to church so much. Not only was I growing spiritually, I was also connecting with friends who went to other schools. The importance of church was communicated to us simply by going each week."

Her advice to busy parents: "Be sure that God is at the center of every decision, and always make time for God and family."

One Family's Spiritual Journey

A newspaper colleague and his wife listen for the voice of God in guiding their busy family through life's tough decisions, including major career and relocation decisions. Their story reminds me anew of the importance of discovering and following God's plan for your life, knowing God helps you in decisions large and small. Study God's words, and think about actions you have taken to follow God, as well as areas where you may have gone off on your own. That same colleague says, "One of the biggest requirements when we moved was that we find a ministry geared to the children's age level. When we first got here, they were ages six, eight, and ten. We visited several churches that did not have an active children's ministry. But the one we found is nothing short of extraordinary." As his children have grown in that church, they have learned to serve others and to have a great time with church friends, participating in activities ranging from mission trips to social outings. "Church activities are supplemented by involvement in school clubs that we monitor closely. We want them to be kids and to have a range of experiences that allow them to be teens. We would never deprive them of that. When you impart God's word into the lives of children, it becomes a way of life.

"Do they make mistakes? They are kids, aren't they? But when there is a misstep, they know that it is up to them to enter back into God's grace. And when we find that they have taken on too much, we have no problem helping them prioritize. Faith guides everything about our family. What we've learned as a family is that God is a lot of fun. He has a wonderful sense of humor. While he expects us to abide by his word, he also wants us to enjoy life now—to hurry less and worry less. There is nothing that we do as a family, no place we would ever go, without having first asked the critical question: are we in the perfect will of God?"

The Church's Help in Tough Times

Developing a spiritual life and connecting with a church helps when things are hard. One young couple struggled to have a child and found comfort in church during that process. "Being unable to have a baby for so long was really a reminder that we aren't in control. We had so many prayers for hope and peace and really needed the spiritual support," he says.

His wife agrees. "Our church is important to us, especially our Sunday school class. We met a great group of people to learn and fellowship with. Our faith in, and relationship with, the Lord makes church and having relationships with Christians important to us. We were both raised going to church and in Christian homes, and we want the same for our son. We want him to learn about Jesus and to develop a personal relationship with him once he is ready."

Volunteering and the Causes You Choose

Many parents want to give back to the community as part of their spiritual life, in an effort to be good stewards of all they have been given. They also want to impart this lesson to their children. Often the requests and even the desire to serve slam right up against other family commitments. As part of your family's rhythm, you will have to consider your own volunteer jobs and commitments. This is a good time to decide how much time you have to offer others.

Many factors—from your work schedule to the ages of your children—go into this. One couple, both members of whom are active volunteers, say they have had to make a change. "We absolutely draw boundaries with our community work. This was not always the case, but now our priority must be family, which leaves little time. Because we have been so active, this is difficult. Most of our volunteer work centers on our faith. There is just not enough time or energy not to focus on the main thing."

Choices can be made with much prayer and communication with your spouse, and also with your children, depending on their ages. "My husband and I feel very strongly about volunteering as a family now that everyone is a little older," one mother says. "We try to take on one thing we can all do together. I want to model for my children what it means to have a giving spirit, and that it's important to give back to your church, your community, your family." She shapes her individual volunteer time around children's activities as much as possible.

A father confesses that he and his wife have "suffered the ill effect of over-volunteering. We both have a very difficult time saying no. We have gotten somewhat better about talking to each other and praying before taking on more responsibilities."

When you consider volunteer opportunities, do not forget to take into account the time they will take you away from your family. While you need adult time and are called to serve others, you want to keep from overloading. "Most opportunities are genuine and have great merit," another father says. "I now look at the real costs in terms of time away from my current commitment. If the commitment takes me off-task in any of the priority areas, then regardless of the merits, I decline."

And from another dad: "I have finally mastered the art of saying no. I used to accept every appointment and was never very good at any of them. Now I only accept invitations that I know I can fulfill. Most of the volunteer work my family does is through our church. There is more than enough to do. The work is never done."

Endless situations will arise that will draw your time and attention. Your children will be exposed to many difficult choices, just as you are. Sit down as a family and talk about the power of God. Give thanks for Christ and grace. Commit your family and all of its confusion and joy to the Lord.

"Choose for yourselves this day whom you will serve. . . . But as for me and my household, we will serve the LORD" (Joshua 24:15). Not a bad priority, is it? Memorize this verse or write it on a piece of paper to stick on your computer or your refrigerator. Go forth with that in mind.

Questions to Consider as You Go Forward

- What is your biggest challenge in talking with your family about faith?
- What small step can you take to guide your family spiritually?
- How might your church involvement need to change?

A PRAYER FOR YOUR JOURNEY

Dear Creator, thank you for grace and forgiveness. Please show me how to help my family know and love you more. Please help each of us know your will for our life and use our gifts to be the people you would have us be. Your gifts are so precious, God, and I thank you; in the name of Jesus. Amen.

Observations from Busy Families

"I try to attend church with my grandkids when I visit. Their immediate family members are not 'frequent flyers' at church, and I want the kids to be exposed to that greatest and most wonderful story of our Savior's love and provision for us. I so want them to have community like only church community can be."

"Sundays were a highlight of the week. We'd dress up for church, fill a pew at morning Mass, then walk to Grandmother's house for a big family meal. To this day, years after my grandparents' deaths, I consider Sunday morning time for faith and family."

"Having the presence of a church life is key in creating a loving home environment. I cannot imagine what our home life would have been like for our children if we had not had our church."

Quick Tip

"There are a few tricks I use to help keep things less hectic. I prepare some home-cooked dishes that make several meals and easily double. When I make these, I often make a dish for our family to eat that week, one to freeze, and then one to give away. I've found it quite handy to have a home-cooked meal ready for a family in need."

Chapter Six

BALANCING HOME
AND WORK

Encouraging Word: *You can get your work under control.*
Everyday Step: *Write family activities on your work
calendar.*

I can do everything through him who gives me strength.
—Philippians 4:13

A smart, cheerful colleague came to work mortified. She
had left the house so harried that morning that she gave her
young daughter a Popsicle for breakfast. "A Popsicle—for
breakfast," she said, over and over. A devoted mom, she had
lost control of the start of that day, trying to make it to a
meeting on time.

In the circus of everyday life, juggling home life and work
life is in the center ring. This topic and the many decisions
surrounding it consume most parents.

Parents know how difficult it is to keep all the balls in the
air. Perhaps you love your work. Or you work out of necessity. Maybe you have chosen to stay at home or to reenter the
workforce after taking time off for a while with your children. Maybe changes in the economy have shaken your
plans; and on and on.

Throw into this mix the often-messy topic of money, and you have a family challenge indeed. Two themes rise above others when the topic of balancing home and work comes up: wanting to spend more time with family, and struggling to make ends meet. Moms and dads make tough decisions day in and day out about the work they do, the money they spend, and the trade-offs they negotiate.

Putting home first may seem like a dream or wishful thinking, but it can work with daily focus. Most of us believe this, but the gap between knowing and doing is often wide. Even thinking about it can cause fatigue. How I wish there were easy ways to handle this, so that you could get it right once, and that would be that. However, having written about this for years and having talked with thousands of people seeking answers, I know that the solutions are often complicated.

The encouraging news is that basic steps help manage this tension better and help you make decisions down the line. You can learn to keep the Big Picture in mind—the importance of your family blended with the value of your work. Grab strategies that work for the career you have chosen and the family life you value. Look for ways to make this process work for you. Do not try to do it all.

As one father reminds, "All the success in the world of work means nothing if you look up and realize that you have missed big chunks of your kids' growing up."

Trying to blend home and work causes guilt. Parents are torn between providing financially for their children, offering their talents to the world, and having more time at home.

As you consider what you want to do, keep your unique situation in mind. You may be called to do special work that is intense and requires odd hours. Or you may be in a season of time when you need to work extra hours to help your company or to supply necessities for your family.

People do best when their commitment to their families is clear. They do not have to choose between their jobs and their families, but they must always try to put families first.

The Work You Choose

Managing the pull of home and work can be easier if you do work that you enjoy and feel called to do. Lots of people start out in a job because they like it or have gifts to do it well. Through the years, they sometimes lose sight of that.

"I love my job," says a mother who coordinates community events for a large hospital. "It's never the same from one day to the next, and I get to make a difference in people's lives on a regular basis." She strives to be an example of having a good work ethic and to teach her children to be the best they can be, and she hopes that they will put God first in all they do.

However, she admits to the regular battle, saying that after her first child was born, "I continued to work out of necessity; and then when the second child came so quickly, there was no question that my salary was needed. It's not all fun and games; I struggle constantly with guilt. I feel guilty when there is something my kids really would like for me to do at their school and I can't because of work. Often things are neglected at work because of sick children or busy children or something. This doesn't cause guilt, it just adds a little anxiety to the mix."

The mother of a toddler is adjusting to having a child and continuing to work at a job that enriches her: "I feel like my work is sort of my mission. The nature of my job is one where I get to see every day the positive difference I am making in people's lives. Whether it is with youth or adults, we are having an impact. I get to help people try to become better citizens and serve and assist them with their needs."

Your approach to work can have a big influence on your children, helping them choose a vocation, shaping the way they will feel someday about their work, and overall affecting their enjoyment of daily life. Throughout the Bible, there are lessons about "eagerly" doing our work and "working with eager hands": "There is nothing better for mortals than to eat and drink, and find enjoyment in their toil. This also, I saw, is from the hand of God" (Ecclesiastes 2:24 NRSV). Work, God says, is not to be done grudgingly.

"I love my work and wake up inspired and ready to go to work," says a social worker and administrator. "I do not let my work affect my home life because when I am home, I am home. I rarely answer the phone when I am home with my kids. The television does not come on much, and I do things like make sure we have dinner together as a family. We work on homework, play with puzzles, take long baths with bubbles, and cuddle to read every night. All of these things help me to recharge with my children, but also disallow negative emotions from work to creep into my home life."

A child development director married to a pastor says, "I feel very blessed to have a partner with a similar calling to serve others and to serve God in our vocations. This is a blessing because we are able to support each other and process part of our demanding jobs together."

"Whatever your task, put yourselves into it, as done for the Lord and not for your masters" (Colossians 3:23 NRSV).

Attending Activities

To deal with the juggling act, be proactive.
Identify the most important activities, those you definitely

do not want to miss. Put those activities on your calendar as early as possible, and plan time off if required.

Consider big events, such as the first day of school, when you are likely to need more time to get things going.

"This is one of the most difficult things for me—if I miss a child's event because of work or have to work on a weekend, or if there is work that needs attention and I can't get to it because of children's activities. I struggle with guilt over this on a regular basis," confesses one mother. Many others echo her words.

"For me, the hardest thing has been balancing work and family," says a new mother. "My job is very demanding at times, and I am expected to be at night meetings, work on some weekends, and spend several nights away from my family on work-related trips. I don't like being away from my husband and baby, but the flexibility I have in my job the rest of the time helps to balance it."

Search your work schedule for flexibility. Some employers are willing to let employees leave work to attend a school play, for example, and then make the time up.

"We prioritize as much as possible," says one couple in Louisiana. "The important things are to ensure that the kids feel safe and secure and have opportunities to achieve their dreams. We both have sacrificed professional promotions to keep that balance."

If you own a business or are the boss, take into account the needs of your employees and their families. Often when people know they have leeway in being with their children at important times, they are happier in what they do, and are more productive and loyal.

A retired city official explains how he handled this: "I tried hard to keep parents from feeling guilty about asking for time off to go to special events in their kids' lives. One hour out of the workweek just did not make that much difference in productivity. In fact, I always believed that I could ask more of those employees when crunch time came, because they knew I'd let them have time for their families at other times of the year."

Leaving Work at Work

Taking work home can be tempting. With today's technology and economic demands, it is easy for parents to work at home or almost anywhere else. Set boundaries for when you will work and when you will be off. Learn to be present with your family at certain times of the day and to avoid being distracted by e-mail or tethered to your cell phone.

"We really do try to leave work at the door and let family time be the center of our attention when we are at home," one parent says. "My husband and I try to keep our work away from our family time and home time. We do not work from home in the evenings unless there is an extenuating circumstance, and we try to keep Saturday as a family day. We plan special family outings and write them on our calendars, so that we do not over-schedule our lives without planning for family fun."

One father uses a similar strategy: "This may sound a bit unusual, but I put all family events on my office calendar. I have told my family that the things on my calendar are my priorities. *They*, my family members, are priorities, and their events need to be listed so that I can make sure not to schedule anything else for that time."

Consider this businessman's story: "I don't allow my frustration with anything going on at the office to enter into my home. I insist that my family sit down together every night, if not for dinner, then just for conversations. Within minutes, we usually laugh loudly, and the troubles of the work-world seem far away. Don't take the stress of work home with you. It's unfair to your family. To them, you are 'Daddy.' That's who they want to see. I am far from perfect, and sometimes the weight of work situations makes this very difficult. But it is something I practice daily. I invite them to tell me when they feel that I am distant and unavailable to them."

Moving On

Another job decision you may be called upon to make is whether to relocate. In my years as a newspaper executive, I saw many friends struggle with this issue. Relocating can bring many joys, including new opportunities and all sorts of adventures. It can also be tough on your family, depending on the ages of your children. You must decide if the advantages of a move are greater than the disadvantages, and how the move fits into your overall family goals. Even in the best of situations, these often cause extra stress and require much family communication.

In choosing, consider your dreams and the needs of your family.

A real estate broker relocated when her daughter was a teen, and then again to live closer to her daughter when she was grown. "Ultimately, every choice you make, whether it's to further your education, change jobs, or just move to another area, impacts your family life. Children adjust very quickly. My daughter was fourteen when we moved to another state, a move she did not want to make. But once school started and she made friends, she was fine. You have to follow your heart."

Another job challenge is deciding how much you will travel or whether you need to make a job change to avoid out-of-town travel. "I could travel constantly based on requests for my services," says a father in the health care industry, "but I choose to try to keep it to a reasonable level because I feel that it is important for stability. I still travel too much for work."

A former colleague tells of a time when she badly wanted to attend a six-week training course on the West Coast to prepare for a computer system installation. At that same time, she got the opportunity to have another foster child in her home. She knew that taking the child would nix any chance of attending the training, but she also knew that welcoming foster children was part of her family mission. She decided to forgo the training course so that she could focus on welcoming the child into her home. "Looking back, I would do it over in a heartbeat. What a joy it has been to see him grow up."

Financial Decisions

The need for money is a heavy load for many families. In some homes, one parent is gone, and providing the means of support falls to a solo parent. In other homes, both parents work and still barely manage to cover basic expenses. In some families, sacrifices are made to give up extras or luxuries. In nearly every instance, when one parent decides to stay home, finances are a factor. Making that decision is tough and often can be a source of conflict with couples. Dealing with relocation or changing jobs can add to that.

"We have two house payments—one for the house we're living in and one for the house we moved from—and other commitments in a state in which we no longer reside," says a parent whose family relocated. "We have children of different ages, all of whom have different needs, including one who needs everything provided for her. My husband has a demanding job, and the economy adds an intangible amount of stress."

The economy goes up and down, and being able to get a handle on your finances can greatly reduce worry. Try to keep the subject in perspective, and call to mind God's view: "Do not store up for yourselves treasures on earth, where moth and rust consume and where thieves break in and steal; but store up for yourselves treasures in heaven. . . . For where your treasure is, there your heart will be also" (Matthew 6:19-21 NRSV).

- Be aware of what you have coming in and going out. Keep your expenses under control.
- Try not to fret about money, especially in front of your children.
- Teach your children how to handle money and the importance of knowing how much something costs and limiting what they buy.
- Trust God to provide, and offer part of your income back to God. Teach your children to do likewise. The reality is that you will often trade money for time or time for money. That decision will require prayer, conversation, and soul searching. As one father says, "Work always seems to come first. My wife, who is also a student, is working part-time, and I am working a more family-oriented shift (eight hours during the day). We sacrificed quite a bit monetarily to spend more time with our children. I don't know how much longer we can continue to do that. It is very tempting to want to go back to making the money we were making before."

Money is a major stressor, and it can make decisions about home and work harder. "Trust in the LORD with all your heart, and do not rely on your own insight. / In all your ways acknowledge him, and he will make straight your paths" (Proverbs 3:5-6 NRSV).

Try to look at your work from a different perspective.

List good things about your job.

Take a hard look at family finances to understand where your money goes.

If you need help, many churches offer excellent courses on money management and can teach you about spending wisely.

Choosing to Stay at Home

Some parents decide to leave the paid workforce while raising children. Others work part-time. These decisions are tough for some, and clearer for others. Here are some examples.

- A Florida mother: "We chose for me to stay home. I wouldn't have had the ability to work and maintain the kind of family life I envisioned. It has been a simple choice for me to stay home. As the children have gotten older, it has been a harder choice to decide to go to work to bring in extra money for vacations and such."
- From another family: "My husband and I both came from families of divorce. When we were young, our mothers were not at home with us after we came home from school each day. When my husband and I were first married, I worked, but when our son was six months old, we decided that I needed to stop working. That's not to say that we didn't need the money. But it was a conscious choice we made for me to be a stay-at-home mom. We don't live in a fancy house or drive the best car, but our children have all their needs met."

- A father's observations: "The single most important choice that has shaped our family was not a choice that I made or ever would have considered making. Shortly after the birth of our first child, my wife chose to leave the 'for-pay' workforce and stay home with our child. As the son of a woman who worked her entire life, I assumed (as did my wife) that she would have a career outside the home. Her choice created opportunities for our children that they otherwise could not have had: one-on-one time during tender years; flexibility to accommodate my demanding work schedule; and the opportunity to be involved in the children's school activities, especially homework and projects. My family understands that having Mom at home is a luxury that not all can choose to have. As such, the entire family understands the value of this."

Part-time Work

One young couple decided that the wife would work part-time after their first child was born. They trimmed their spending to make it happen. "The amount of time I work is perfect for me to be able to feel like I'm making a difference in the community," the woman says. "It's not about what I want to do anymore. It's about our son. And the love you have for this other little person is amazing!"

Approaches vary greatly, depending upon family situations. "When I was pregnant, it never occurred to me that I couldn't work full-time and be a mom. However, that was before the sleepless nights and lack of energy," says a mother of three. She took time off with the birth of each child and then went back to teaching part-time. "I have come to realize that each parent is different in terms of comfort level in parenting. I would have gone crazy staying at home. I need some kind of adult interaction outlet. I realized when I stayed home with my second child that a good part of my identity came from being a teacher, and I did not seem to find my niche as a stay-at-home mom. I'm a terrible housekeeper, and I was quite depressed cleaning the house only to see it messed up again and again."

Another family is a good example of how fluid the journey can be. The wife and her husband make adjustments as needed to live by their priorities. "In all that we do, we consider our family first. Our choice for me to go back to work when our daughter was a baby was quite difficult," the mother says. "I spent many months in prayer. I felt so guilty for leaving my little one for others to care for." Later, "we chose for me to leave a full-time teaching position to take a part-time job at church. Yes, there were financial sacrifices, but that was the simple part. I was spending more time with our sweet daughter." When they had a son, work shifted again: "It took almost a year to finally decide to stay at home. Again, because of the economy, we have had to cut back financially and make some sacrifices. What we are not sacrificing is our valuable time with our children. They will not miss out on material things; I do believe they would be missing out on time with us."

Talk with people whom you know and trust for ideas on what might work best for you and your family. Do not beat yourself up if your way is not the same as someone else's. Look for ways to make it work, no matter how hard it may seem.

Consider the home in which you grew up and the approach your parents had. What did you like about it, and what do you want to do differently? Visit with friends and ask about their experiences. Create something unique and special for your family.

"I grew up in the 1950s and 1960s believing that girls could achieve or accomplish as much as boys," says the daughter of physicians. "Mother was a powerful example, of course. But my father's deep love for her spoke clearly that a woman did not have to sacrifice having a family in order to have a career. Dad was immensely proud of her."

My own mother worked for as long as I can remember. It was hard work, and it did not pay well. But through her work, she taught my brothers and me about integrity, persistence, the value of education, and about making sacrifices for others. These lessons have served us well, and you may find that the hardest choices you make will help your children become the people they were created to be.

Help from Others

For most working parents, outside help of some kind is needed, especially the support of friends and relatives. For parents who live close to their own parents or siblings, often the answer is easier.

"My mother has helped me immensely," says a single working mom. "I could not have made it through grad school without her babysitting. All through the years I never had to pay for a babysitter because of her. Plus, she and my daughter had a great relationship. She was my daughter's favorite person; they always had fun together. My mother also bought things for her without my asking her, which was a big help too."

"Having a great caregiver after school when the kids are little is a godsend," says the mother of adopted and foster children. "Don't be too proud to accept help."

One of my favorite perspectives on dealing with busy times came from a friend in middle school. What does her family do when things get too hectic with two babies and a teen? "We call in more family to help."

When All Is Said and Done

When you get home from work, you need energy to meet your children's needs. Try to allow a few moments to refresh yourself, a ritual that helps you shift gears. I well recall my mother coming home, changing out of her work uniform, and having a cup of coffee and a slice of bread. It was her way of transitioning to the evening.

Seek ways to connect with your children, to inquire about their day, and to engage with them, even if you are tired. As one church worker and parent says, be "hands-on, involved, and intentional about planning 'talking time.'" That includes time to talk together as a family about friends, feelings, and other issues.

I love the following account from a schoolteacher, a mother whose daughter now lives half a country away: "I always seemed to ask myself if I had saved enough energy and excitement for my own child after giving so much to my schoolchildren during the day. It would have been so easy to have said 'I'm too tired' or 'I have housework to do' when she wanted to build a tent in the living room, read a book, or pull out the art supplies to paint a picture. Luckily, my husband swooped in to allow me a bit of time to cook supper while he played with our daughter, or he would cook while I played. It was great teamwork that allowed each of us to have time with her, besides our time as a family. I think our children deserve as much time as we can give—when we are tired, when we are overwhelmed, and when we are fresh and full of vigor."

And as another working mother says, "Personal goals are not as important as my children's well-being."

The choices are difficult, and resolve often is required.

"I decided a long time ago that family came first. This is hard, but it was a sacrifice I was willing to make. It was a hard choice because I am such a perfectionist. I want to be perfect at work and at home, but I realized that as long as I take care of home, the rest of it will work out," says one parent.

Give up worries, and do what you need to do for your family. "Cast all your anxiety on him, because he cares for you" (1 Peter 5:7 NRSV).

Questions to Consider as You Go Forward

- What do you enjoy about your work?
- How does your family benefit from your job?
- What one step could you take to juggle work and home life better?

A PRAYER FOR YOUR JOURNEY

Dear Heavenly Lord, you know the many things I juggle each day and my need for your help with my schedule. Please give me wisdom in my day's activities and help me make smart decisions. Show me the right choices to make regarding work; in the name of Christ. Amen.

Observations from Busy Families

"Don't try to keep up with the Joneses. You don't really know what their life is like."

"In tough lines of work, sacrifice a day's work if possible. Start with a half-day if need be, but work four long days instead of five if possible."

"Being a single parent was difficult. Having a second person to reinforce what you are doing and just have your back makes a difference. But every day there are women and men who do the same thing and are successful parents."

Quick Tip

"Slow down. You can't do everything."

Chapter Seven

WHEN HARD TIMES
COME ALONG

Encouraging Word: *Don't be afraid to ask for help.*
Everyday Step: *Strike an item off your "worry" list.*

> *I cry aloud to the LORD;*
> *I lift up my voice to the LORD for mercy.*
> *I pour out my complaint before him;*
> *before him I tell my trouble.*
> *When my spirit grows faint within me,*
> *it is you who know my way.*
> *—Psalm 142:1-3*

*I*t's not as bad as it seems."

"It won't last forever."

"Persevere. God is faithful."

Those words of advice for tough times come from a father who has encountered a variety of daily challenges. The simplicity of these words offers hope for other parents trying to make it through the wilderness of family crises and drama. This message also serves as a steady reminder for each person who hits a speed bump.

Everyday life places a variety of demands on families. Illness strikes. Tragedy occurs. Loved ones die. Parents grow apart and divorce. Children get in trouble at school. The list is long, and everyone you know likely has been touched by pain. Maybe today it is even you, your life, your family.

In addition to big crises, there are the myriad small problems and concerns that keep parents awake at night. Anyone who lets a child or grandchild head out into the world knows that feeling—the prayers you've prayed for their safety, the concern you have for their return.

Learn to replace worry with trust. Start to believe that things will turn out for the best.

Trying to tackle everything at once can be overwhelming. Break your worries and problems into bite-sized pieces. You can move forward, whether you are feeling ashamed at how angry you have been with your children or whether you are watching your own parent drift away with a life-threatening illness.

We gain encouragement from those around us and often need a shoulder to cry on. Turn to friends and family. Ask for their love and prayers. Pray for others.

One of the great reassurances of the Bible is that God is with us every day. "I will go before you / and level the mountains," we are told in Isaiah (45:2 NRSV). Those words come in handy. On some days the mountains can seem insurmountable.

Most people worry about their children, no matter their ages. And they worry about their own abilities to lead and guide and to be the best parent possible. But this worry erodes the joy of daily life. Instead of focusing on what is working, too often we focus on what is going wrong or what *might* go wrong.

Despite daily challenges and bad times, you will be helped by a positive outlook and trust in God. As one young father says, "I'm still struggling with realizing there is only so much we can do. It's really in God's hands."

At some level, many of us know that—we *believe* it, even. But it is hard to practice in daily life. I frequently refer to a biblical parenting story found in Mark 9, the account of a troubled father who brought his ill son to Jesus. The father said, " 'If you can do anything, take pity on us and help us.' ' "If you can"?' said Jesus. 'Everything is possible for him who believes.' Immediately the boy's father exclaimed, 'I do believe; help me overcome my unbelief!' " (vv. 22-24).

Perhaps you find such a paradox in your own parenting life. You believe, and yet you struggle with worries about your children. Once those worries start, they often grow.

"I worry about my child's well-being and health," says the mother of a toddler. "I worry that he will not be successful or happy. I worry that other children will not like him. I worry that I will not provide all I can for my child."

Who Worries?

Nearly everyone seems to worry, despite our realization that it doesn't solve problems. This habit afflicts rich and poor, those who are employed and those who stay at home. It keeps mothers up at night and causes fathers to toss and turn.

"People sometimes suggest that those living in poverty do not worry as much about their children as middle-class or affluent families, but this is unequivocally untrue," says the director of a nonprofit center. "All parents have the same worries and concerns regarding time: Am I spending enough time with my child? Is that quality time? Are my children getting what they need from me? Are my children developing and growing at a normal pace like other children? Am I doing enough? These are all questions parents bring to me. As the economy has worsened, the trends have been more toward worries about economic stressors, for all people I come in contact with—those I serve at my job, as well as church members and friends."

The Issue of Money

Most of us have given ourselves *the talking to*—the one where we remind ourselves that we are greatly blessed, and that many people have it worse than us.

But even though you may have tried to push them away, the worries about money can keep nudging at you.

This spills over from the conversation about home and work, and it adds another layer of worry to that sometimes-tense situation. The bills often seem to arrive more quickly than the checks, and families have to find ways to adjust.

Gather specific facts to help you manage your money better, and, thus, to handle your money woes. Figure out how much money you actually have. Go through your expenses. Use the difference—either negative or positive—to make hard choices, from the amount you will save to a plan to get out of debt.

Cut back on your spending if you are in debt. Work out a budget, and don't buy things you cannot afford. Try to help your children understand financial realities, while not drawing them into adult worries.

The Saddest of Times

Sometimes awful things happen that make other worries pale in comparison. Turning to God for mercy often is the only way to make it through these times. This I have heard from a multitude of people, including those who have faced those most tragic of losses, the loss of a child or a spouse.

Many parents in the Bible encountered this need for mercy, such as this story of a father, a leader in the synagogue, who begged Jesus to heal his daughter. " 'My little daughter is at the point of death. Come and lay your hands on her, so that she may be made well, and live.' So he went with him" (Mark 5:22-24 NRSV). Jesus told the father, "Do not fear, only believe" (v. 36). And Jesus called the father and mother together as he restored the girl to life, in what was surely a tender family moment.

Perhaps you find yourself in deep pain and do not know where to turn. Reflect on these verses of Scripture:

"In my distress I called to the LORD, / and he answered me," says Jonah 2:2a.

"I lift up my eyes to the hills— / where does my help come from? / My help comes from the LORD, / the Maker of heaven and earth" (Psalm 121:1-2).

"Who shall separate us from the love of Christ? Shall trouble or hardship or persecution or famine or nakedness or danger or sword? . . . No, in all these things we are more than conquerors through him who loved us. For I am convinced that neither death nor life, neither angels nor demons, neither the present nor the future, nor any powers, neither height nor depth, nor anything else in all creation, will be able to separate us from the love of God that is in Christ Jesus our Lord" (Romans 8:35, 37-39).

Call upon words such as these to help you through the saddest of times and to help you put the pieces of your life back together. Ask God to bring you peace. Know that though your pain may not go away, it will become manageable.

The mother of two sons experienced the death of an infant son and describes coping, saying she has learned to be more aware of others in pain. "The only words of encouragement I can give is to say that you will make it through even when you swear you won't. But I would also be honest and say that the pain never goes away. You just learn to cope with it and continue living."

Talk Through Tough Situations

You will through the years be called upon to make hard decisions about how to share concerns with your children. You will want to be honest with them, but you must remember that they are your children.

"It's important that parents not lose sight of the fact their children can sense anxiety, and it can negatively impact their life. While children need to see realism, they do not have to experience adult stress," says a father. "Having a safe place for them to slow down and be heard is invaluable."

"I've seen lots of friends and families go through really hard times," says a student. "Whether it is simply not getting along or something as life changing as the loss of a loved one, it is so important to communicate with your family. My friend called me over a school break crying because her mother had just yelled at her for not spending enough time at home. Her mother's yelling made my friend angry and upset, and my friend wasn't able to see where her mother was coming from until she calmed down and they talked. Communication is key."

Use the rough times to remind you, too, of the value of your family, to help you communicate the love you have.

"My older brother died when I was ten years old," says a mother of teens. "Two of my friends lost their young children in accidents. You don't know how long you will have someone. Touch them, hug them, love them. Not a day goes by that I don't think about my lost loved ones. What I wouldn't do for one more touch, one more 'I love you.' "

An expert in family development says that those who encounter hardships often are brought together as a family. "Through my experiences, many times it seems that the families who have more struggles or who have been handed a tougher time in life are able to find a way to come through with a better outlook than those families who may not have had to struggle."

"Keep the lines of communication open," says one grandmother. "Be frank with your children, and let them know as much as they can understand at their age levels. A teen will understand a parent's job layoff and its implications better than a five-year-old, but the young child deserves to know *something*—otherwise, she may think that she's the cause of the problem. This is especially important when someone has to take a job in another location and leave the family, even temporarily. The same is true of military personnel scheduled for deployment. Children are amazingly resilient. As long as they feel secure in the family's love, they can weather almost anything. Keeping communication open also means children will come to a parent with questions, will be able to ask the hard questions, and will trust the parent for good advice."

The Everyday World

Many parents are concerned about preparing their children to deal with temptations and tough times in the world. They worry about this quite a lot. As one father says, "As the kids have gotten older, I have seen outside influences starting to affect their opinions and behaviors. I am a realist in that I know this is a challenge for all parents, and no matter how much you wish to protect them from negative influences, you cannot hide your children away from the world. I just pray that we provide our children with the moral and ethical foundation that will serve them the rest of their lives."

Balancing your family's values and those of the world around you can be one of the biggest challenges of parenting. "We want our children to be aware of others' needs and to look for ways to help," says the mother of two. "And we want them to be strong enough to stand up to fight for what is right. Not being in control of their lives as much as we were when they were younger is getting tough for us. We are seeing this as our daughter gets older. The adventure continues."

Figure out the lessons you want to impart to your children, whether it is teaching them how to make good decisions, the value of always being honest, or the importance of faith. You might even make a list of these and other important lessons to clarify your thinking. Consider how to communicate these lessons to your children; you will find this to be a much more positive approach than worrying.

Be involved in your children's lives—know who their friends are, keep up with where they are, and stay plugged in to their schoolwork. Such little efforts can help ease worries along the way and prevent major problems.

"We, as parents, often get very wound up and worried about things that are really not that important at all—magnet school testing, having the right clothing, getting invited to the right birthday party, having a huge birthday party for a five-year-old. These days, I am a little more laid back," says the mother of two. "Don't get me wrong. I certainly worry over my children often and want the best for them, but I also want them to know what really matters in life: Are we kind to others? Do we love and respect ourselves? What are we doing to make the world better? I believe that even a five-year-old can be taught how he or she can make the world better. So I try to take things as they come at me, remember that I cannot control things, and try to make good decisions."

The Teen Years

Make an effort not to be anxious about the teen years. If your children are young, work each day to communicate with them and to build a strong relationship, as you teach them right from wrong. Have fun with them and love them, and build a bridge that you can walk over when they move into their teen years.

"I'm so afraid of those years and all the things that are out there for them. That's going to be really hard," says one mom, voicing what many parents feel. This might be a good time to remind yourself not to anticipate that things will go wrong. Keep doing your best with your children, and trust that they will make good choices as they mature.

The Bible has good parenting advice for this: "Do not be anxious about anything, but in everything, by prayer and petition, with thanksgiving, present your requests to God. And the peace of God, which transcends all understanding, will guard your hearts and your minds in Christ Jesus" (Philippians 4:6-7).

If your children are already in their teens, look for ways to build closeness and to help them make good decisions. And if your children are older, look back on the good times and put the regrets to rest.

"I hear parents of pre-teen children often expressing worry that they are at high risk of losing their children to all the bad things in the world, such as alcohol, drugs, and sex, and they fear they will lose their kids forever," says the mother of two young adults. "This worry keeps them from enjoying the great times they are having with their kids currently, and if the parents express this fear to the kids, the kids themselves can begin to fear their teen years rather than look forward to the joys they will bring.

"The likelihood of good kids going wrong is actually quite low. The stronger the bond between young kids and parents, the less likely it is that kids will wander far from the nest in regard to a change in behavior and values. Sure, they may be searching for their identity and become unrecognizable at times, but basically they are still the wonderful children they were when they were younger. They will emerge on the other side of their teen years as fabulous young adults—if parents don't make too much out of the day-to-day conflicts."

Caring for Older Parents

My parents both died young. But when I go through a list of my close friends, many of them are caring for aging parents who are ill, suffering from dementia, or merely slowing down and needing extra care. As I watch my friends, I see an immense load that they bear, even from those things they do with great love. They must find ways to work in doctors' visits and medicine pick-ups, and patiently sit and visit even when they have other demands and anticipate the worry of legal and financial issues.

Being a loving adult child of older parents is a responsibility and an honor, and a season of time that an increasing number of people are entering. Some even feel as though the roles are reversing, as they find themselves taking care of their parents and other aging relatives. This adds to the busyness of family life.

Caring for parents often brings a stream of worry and frustration. A friend e-mailed me about the demands of caring for an elderly aunt while working and taking care of her own children. These demands that she faced required her to reconsider her list of volunteer commitments and to make decisions about which activities to eliminate. Perhaps you need to make similar adjustments.

If you depend upon a sibling to help care for a parent or other relative, give them a break too. "Step in and relieve the family members who are in town," says a woman whose mother and mother-in-law are in poor health. "Do not make your visit to town a social event. Give them a day off." She continues with more advice for those who do most of the care giving: "Do not hesitate to ask the family members who live out of town to help. The family members who live in town carry a huge daily burden. It is good for those who live out of town to realize they can help carry the load."

And be there for your spouse, to ease the load. "Help each other out," this same woman says. "Sometimes my husband takes care of his mother. Sometimes I step in and take care of her."

A woman who cared for both of her parents in the latter years of their lives learned the joy of living in the moment during these often-difficult days: "Cherish the opportunity to relate to them adult to adult, instead of parent to child. Share your life—the challenges you face, the people you meet, the funny things that happen. This perspective may actually help you deal with problems."

And remember this passage: "Children, obey your parents in the Lord, for this is right. 'Honor your father and mother'—this is the first commandment with a promise: 'so that it may be well with you and you may live long on the earth.' And, fathers, do not provoke your children to anger, but bring them up in the discipline and instruction of the Lord" (Ephesians 6:1-4 NRSV).

Seek Outside Help

Sometimes you may not be able to handle the stress of parenting. Do not hesitate to seek help. You may find that a trusted friend, relative, or other parent can be the ear you need. But you may need professional help—from a pastor or counselor or doctor. Do not let your questions, frustrations, and problems go unheeded.

A professional counselor suggests asking for help when needed: "For some reason, we seem to think we can do this enormous job of parenting without any instructions or help because everyone else seems to be doing it. Children do not come with a manual, but there is a huge need for parent training for all of us." This counselor also offers some guidelines for when and where to seek outside help: "Parents should look for help when they realize that what they are doing is not very effective; definitely when they feel frustrated, tired, and overwhelmed; and when the child's behavior worsens or there are problems in school. Most elementary schools offer classes or information about classes. Doctors and churches are also a good resource. So are online sites, books, school counselors, and family members."

As another counselor says, "I learn a lot about the dignity and grace with which most people handle hard times. I see those who lose their jobs and have to ask for help. That is difficult, but it is something they have to do to help care for their families. I have learned that different people handle things differently, but mostly they all do the best they can to manage and take care of their families. More often than not I am pleasantly surprised with the human spirit and people's ability to manage difficult things."

Keep looking for answers. Replace fear with faith. Walk through the worst times and come out on the other end. "Rise, let us go!" says Christ in Matthew 26:46.

Questions to Consider as You Go Forward

- What concerns might you turn over to God?
- What fuels your worries? How can you change that?
- What is going right in your life?

A PRAYER FOR YOUR JOURNEY

Dear God, I come to you eager to trust. Strengthen my faith. Please help me put anxieties away and seek positive ways to deal with life's stresses. Help me through times of trial and pain. Watch over my family and those who are in our lives, as we are much in need of your love and mercy; in your name. Amen.

Observations from Busy Families

"Take one day at a time. If a day doesn't go so well, remember that tomorrow is a new day. Remember, the most important thing is to love your child."

"Putting the children first is the key in dealing with divorce. We have to let go of the issues that caused the breakup, no matter how hurtful these issues are. If not, it will only cause problems."

"Don't be afraid to ask for help. It is so good to connect with other parents and to work together in life's big challenges. Parents need to take care of themselves and replenish themselves so they can take care of others. And remember that perfection is a miserable thing to try to attain. It is not real."

Quick Tip

"I've known very few children—babies through adults—who don't like hugs and being told that they are loved."

Chapter Eight

THE SIMPLICITY
OF CONSISTENCY

Encouraging Word: *You can follow through as needed.*
Everyday Step: *Think about what you will say*
before you say it.

Train a child in the way he should go,
and when he is old he will not turn from it.
—Proverbs 22:6

Five rose bushes make their home in our yard—the few plants that are entrusted to my care. They offer great pleasure but require specific kinds of attention, including twice-a-year pruning. Something about that pruning hurts me: they're all "bushed out" and growing, and I'm supposed to snip them back considerably. As I do, I wonder if I'm stunting them; wouldn't it be better to let them flourish, unchecked?

Each year the pruning has spectacular results. The rose bushes branch out quickly, bud, and grow vigorously. The blooms are so pretty. By cutting them back, I've somehow opened them up.

Being a loving and consistent parent is similar to this. Teaching your children to know right from wrong can be hard. Saying no to them can feel like too much pruning.

Not surprisingly, *love* is one of the first words parents mention when talking about family life. But the word *consistent* comes in a close second. The desire to be consistent runs through the veins of many parents, even those who find it nearly impossible to say no to their children.

Parents want consistency in their schedules, their discipline, their attitude, and their time for fun. This bubbles up as a way to make life better for the children, as well as for Mom and Dad. When parents are consistent, they see the benefits—a simplicity to tangled days.

"The best thing I have done as a parent, for me and my daughter, is be consistent," says one woman. "It's not only good for the child, but it makes your life as a parent so much easier." Watching her, I am always touched by how consistent she is with her child, in loving and disciplining when correction is needed.

Even the newest of parents have this on their radar. "My parenting philosophy would be 'laid back and consistent.' I try to be as easygoing as possible and not stress over the small stuff," says a new mother and teacher. "I want my son to be and feel loved and independent, even at a young age. I try to be consistent, but still flexible, with routines such as eating, playing, and how he's put down for sleep."

When You Falter

Despite your best intentions, sometimes you will snap, shout, or say something you regret, and you have to step back, regain your composure, and apologize as needed.

The words of the Apostle Paul in the book of Romans give me hope here, as he struggled with the same thing: "I do not understand what I do. For what I want to do I do not do, but what I hate I do" (Romans 7:15). While Paul wasn't talking about parenting, he certainly could have been!

As one young, working mother asks, "How can I have more of God and reflect him more? I feel that I don't do that, and that who I want to be is not who I am. There has to be a way to reach inside and reflect more, and not feel so cranky."

"My 'new' philosophy is that kids need structure," says a working mother who is also in school. "Bedtime is at 8:00 P.M. on weeknights, and nobody gets to watch TV on school nights. They have to practice their musical instruments every day except the days when they have lessons. Schoolwork and music practice come first every day. Then there is time for talk, family, games, and sharing. Sometimes I think that I may go overboard with this kind of approach, like a prison warden, but I have found that if we don't accomplish our tasks from the beginning of each evening, we run too late in getting to bed."

Weary and Burdened

Being overly busy often leads to fatigue, which can lead to a lack of consistency. These moments of frustration require that you take your own adult timeout—spend a few minutes taking a hot bath, wandering around the yard, reading, or writing in your journal. Plan a quiet time, even if it is only a few minutes' long. Sit in your favorite chair and consider the blessing of the day. Forgive yourself.

Sometimes you are so tired that you think you can't possibly muster the energy to give the children the attention they need or to deal with yet another issue. Know that Christ will refresh you: "Come to me, all you who are weary and burdened, and I will give you rest" (Matthew 11:28).

Deciding on Discipline

Discipline is an ongoing part of a less-hurried, less-worried household, and a huge part of the consistency discussion.

"Many children want and need discipline in a variety of ways," says a child-care provider, mother, and grandmother. "As adults, we need to recognize this, and find loving and creative ways to provide the type of discipline a child needs for that moment or action."

The more rushed a parent is, the more likely he or she is to make a snap decision about discipline or to let a problem go. And parents must work out with their spouse the details of discipline, a topic on which they sometimes disagree. "Often parents are not consistent, and they are reluctant to be firm," says a professional family counselor. "Parents give in a lot because they are tired, because they feel guilty about not having enough time for the kids, or because it is just easier."

Present a united front on discipline and other important matters. The mother of two adult children says, "Knowing that their parents are a united team in all things is a security guarantee for a child. This way, even when he is disciplined and is seemingly mad about it inside, the child senses that he is cared about."

A new father elaborates on this: "We feel as parents that we must be on the same page when disciplining our daughter. If we are not on the same page, how can we expect her to understand our definition of right from wrong? I feel it is my primary responsibility that she understands right from wrong, with a loving and caring but firm and consistent message." This, he says, is his biggest challenge in parenting. His wife agrees: "We want to stay consistent and send the same message."

This part of parenting is what some describe as "a work in progress." One mother says, "Discipline has been a difficult road and continues to be, with my husband and me having grown up with different people using different parenting styles. But we work on this constantly. I have to work very hard at not correcting my husband's decisions in front of the kids. He's really good at not doing that to me, but I fly off the handle a little more often and find myself apologizing, because I do think that it is very bad to contradict each other, both in terms of the approach to discipline itself and in terms of the relationship between husband and wife."

Communicate with your spouse about the decisions you make, and respect each other. "Whenever there is a disagreement on parenting, we usually find a way to compromise or to at least fully discuss the matters," says one parent.

Setting limits can help your children deal better with the world around them and can help them mature into individuals who know how to navigate daily life. Another parent says, "I want my children to remember their childhood as a time when they felt happy, safe, secure, and loved. I want them to feel they had limits on their behavior because it was something that would help them to be better adults. I set guidelines and limits on how we are allowed to behave, and I hold them to those limits."

Help your children learn how to step away from a situation to see it more clearly. Remember, too, that each child is different. "It's humorous but true that although they have been raised under the same roof and exposed to the same parenting skills, their personalities are so different," says a parent in Mississippi. "That requires a different parental management style, if you will, for each one. What motivates one won't work for the others. If you compared it to the workplace, it would be like having three employees who come from different circumstances but who have a common background. Parenting is challenging but thrilling beyond belief. At the end of the day, the kids truly love each other, they love us, and they know that no subject is off-limits for conversation."

Tone of Voice

Sometimes, as one mother says, you have to work to "speak sweetly" with your children. Even when you have to correct them or steer them in a different direction, do that with love and gentleness.

"Love is patient; love is kind; love is not envious or boastful or arrogant or rude. It does not insist on its own way; it is not irritable or resentful" (1 Corinthians 13:4-5 NRSV). Those words are an excellent guide for each part of your daily life—and a good parenting reminder.

Handling Daily Behavior

These perspectives from three different mothers give insight into letting children know what is expected of them:

- "Two things that are not flexible are these: that the kids feel loved, and that I set up a situation before we ever begin it." To do so, this woman talks with her children before they go somewhere or have company, helping them know things they can do, things they should not do, and the consequences if they do the wrong thing. "I noticed that preparing them for situations in advance worked so much better," she says.
- "My style is pure common sense and comes from a deep desire to connect with and simply love my children," a second mother says. "I see parents scream at their children or

say things that shame them, or fail to follow up on consequences, and I wonder about the long-term benefits of such approaches. Of course, I have done all of the above, but I try hard to avoid those behaviors."

- A third mother says, "I believe that whatever it is that you say, you'd better follow through with it. You'd better be careful if you say it. Knowing that I have to follow through makes me stop before I say something, and it makes me more aware. It also keeps me from blowing up just because I'm tired."

Telling Your Children No

Learning to say no to children seems to be about as hard for parents as learning to say no to too many activities. By doing so, however, you can help them simplify their lives and learn to make better decisions. Here is the voice of experience:

- "I refrain from over-scheduling, and if you ask my daughter, I am sure she would say I say no to everything. I try not to let her be away from home several nights a week. I think it helps keep a calm feeling in the house and gives our family some structure."
- "It's OK to tell your children no. Recently, my daughter wanted to go out on a Friday night, and I knew it had been a long week at school. I told her she could go out on Saturday. Her friends weren't very happy with me, but my daughter told me later that she appreciated my telling her no. She needed to rest."
- "I think the biggest challenge is not giving in to every desire of children. Society now makes that really hard. Most people are parenting their children with material

things instead of love and guidance. That is hard for those of us who don't."

• "As your children grow up, they are presented with many opportunities in life," says a parent. "You do your best to guide them to succeed. Sometimes looking at the big picture and saying no to something that sounds fun will bring success in the long run."

Saying no in love can move your child in the right direction. "Keep alert, stand firm in your faith, be courageous, be strong. Let all that you do be done in love" (1 Corinthians 16:13-14 NRSV).

Friendship versus Parenting

A surprising number of parents mention the importance of loving their children but not necessarily being their child's friend. While you are trying to be consistent, you may also walk that fine line of being too chummy with your children.

Listen to these parents as they discuss their efforts. See if you find yourself making similar decisions:

• "Children love structure and age-appropriate boundaries, but a parent must be consistent with those boundaries. I always had to remind myself that I was her parent, not her best friend. She will tell you that she heard over a million times me saying these words: 'God chose me to be your parent, not your best friend.' She has always been the joy of my life, and as a married adult, she has become a dear friend; but as we raised her, we tried to remind ourselves that being a parent was our primary role. We wanted her to respect us, even when she might disagree with us."

- "I think I am able to be a friend to my kids as well as a teacher, counselor, and ethical compass for them. When I say 'friend,' I don't mean that I'm here to party with them and act their age. I mean I am here to talk to them (a lot!) about what they do and think, to let them be who they are meant to be, and to love them for who they are."

- "I've learned what it means when people say you can't be your kid's friend," says one grandmother. "Establishing boundaries and exercising authority comes into play at some point. This has not been as big an issue with my grandparenting as it was with parenting my own kids. In fact, I was practically a kid myself when I had them."

At the end of the day, as one father says, you still have to be their parents, even as they move into high school and beyond: "It became much harder to be both friend and parent to our children. It was more important to be the temporarily unpopular parent than to give in on core decisions. They come and visit often, and we enjoy this new relationship with our adult children."

Do you seek ways to be consistent with your child, to love the child completely while still being a parent who disciplines and guides?

"Trust between parent and child is forged when the child is very young," says one mother. "Giving mixed messages is the worst thing a parent can do. Screaming and yelling one minute, and hugging the child the next only causes confusion. Parents need to realize that discipline can be carried out without drama—but it takes practice and resolve. No one is the perfect parent—I certainly wasn't, and neither was my husband—but we did the best we could. That's all any parent can do."

One-on-one Time

Consistent one-on-one time for each child, where they feel special, is also important. This helps you communicate more deeply and get to know that child better.

Different parents manage this in different ways, and it almost always requires planning. Step back and consider ways to connect with your children as individuals. What are their special interests? What do you have fun doing together?

"Plan outings with one child at a time for more quality time," says the mother of three. This might involve having lunch out and shopping or going to the park or doing a craft. It could also simply mean choosing to read a book together.

"Listen, and love each child unconditionally. Understand their world and enjoy their time at home," says another parent.

"Now that I have two grandchildren, I have much more insight into good parenting. I know that the key is communication, as it is with most things," says a mother in Georgia. "As a working, single parent, there were many times when I did not take the time to talk with my daughter as regularly as I should have. I now realize that simple things such as sitting down to eat together and asking about how her day went are important. We need to keep the door open to talk."

Children want this. As a young parent advises, "Spend time together, and listen when your kids talk to you."

Special Attention

A teacher of troubled students in a large urban area observes "disturbing trends" related to the family, trends that are wrapped up in sadness and hard times: "Disconnected families; excessive pressure applied to children to perform, both athletically and academically; time-management problems; and spiritual voids. I see a lot of troubled students in my classroom whom I believe are direct casualties from some of these trends."

These issues are unsettling and require special kinds of attention. Perhaps you see them in your own household. Professional help may be required as you deal with them, including parents and children visiting with a pastor or a counselor.

More about Unconditional Love

The Bible is full of stories of parents and their love for their children—many of them reminders of how tough the role can be. One of the most moving parenting stories is that of the prodigal son, the lost son who snatched his inheritance early and blew it all. This story, from the Gospel of Luke, is about a child who has "gone bad" and a father's unconditional love.

This story has many layers, deep messages of redemption and forgiveness. It is also about consistency and devotion and juggling the needs of more than one child. When the lost son realized had badly he had messed up, he decided to return home, apologize, and ask for help, and he asked not to be given more as a son, but instead to be treated as an employee. He was desperate. The writer of Luke says, "But while he was still a long way off, his father saw him and was filled with compassion for him; he ran to his son, threw his arms around him and kissed him. The son said to him, 'Father, I have sinned against heaven and against you. I am no longer worthy to be called your son' " (Luke 15:20a-21).

The father welcomed him with an intense love and a celebration. You might imagine how the elder brother, the "good" son who had stayed at home, felt. He was angry and felt slighted. The father stressed his love to both sons. To the faithful son, the elder brother, the father said, "Everything I have is yours. But we had to celebrate and be glad, because this brother of yours was dead and is alive again; he was lost and is found" (Luke 15:31-32).

Perhaps you have children who have strayed. Maybe they have lost their way altogether. Continue to pray for them and to love them. The miracle of redemption may be just down the road.

Love consistently. Teach your children right from wrong. Relax as you watch them blossom. Pray when they wander.

Questions to Consider as You Go Forward

- What changes might you make to be more consistent as a parent?
- What guidelines do you use to discipline your children?
- Have you struggled with the distinction between being a parent and a friend to your child? If so, how? If not, how do you maintain a consistent approach?

A PRAYER FOR YOUR JOURNEY

Dear Loving God, thank you for reminding me of your constant love and tender mercies. Help me share such love with my family and make steady, wise decisions each day. Keep me from wavering, Lord, and guide my family in every way, every day; in the holy name of your Son. Amen.

The Simplicity of Consistency

Observations from Busy Families

"Pray! Be consistent. Rely on your own judgment as well as on the guidance of those whom you respect as good parents and role models. This may include your own parents. Know what you value, and stick to those values in the decisions you make."

"Communicate, and don't let stuff build up until you explode. Don't hold grudges. Show love. Listen. Be patient. Have fun together."

"Make sure your children know how much you love them and how proud you are of them, even when you are at your most upset."

Quick Tip

"We try never to let them fall asleep without a good-night kiss and a hug, tucking them in, and saying prayers together."

117

Chapter Nine

FUN AND
GAMES

Encouraging Word: *Each day offers ways to have fun.*
Everyday Step: *Plan a playful weekend together.*

This is the day the LORD has made;
let us rejoice and be glad in it.
—*Psalm 118:24*

On a sunny winter weekend, several members of my family gathered at a north Louisiana lake. My fifth-grade niece played in the mud with her bright rubber boots. She and a friend explored a nearby island. My niece laughed. She walked amazingly gracefully across a rope-bridge her dad made for her. My middle-aged husband, never deterred by a challenge, gave it a try too. Not so graceful, he still succeeded in avoiding the murky water below. We cooked out, ate chocolate–peanut butter ice cream, watched movies, and even discovered a small parade in a nearby state park.

This was a less-hurried, less-worried weekend for our family. Whew, are they hard to come by!

You probably know it is not easy to put everything aside and play. Such a weekend requires a fair amount of planning

119

and a willingness to let other things go for a while, a juggling of schedules and the logistics of life.

Parents long for this—more fun with their families. For those whose children are older or grown and gone from home, often this is their biggest regret, that they didn't have more relaxed, playful times with their children.

Start now, no matter the season of time you are in or the circumstances of your life. You don't have to start big, but step out. Be relentless about having family time and having fun as a family, creating memories and traditions, sharing activities, and telling family stories.

"When my children look back on their childhood, I hope they remember the time we spent together as a family, whether that involves our evening meals or vacations together," says one mother.

Teach your family members to enjoy each day and to have fun. You will be giving them a gift that will serve them throughout their lives. Christ said he came that we might have life to the full (see John 10:10). I believe this abundant life means savoring each day and having fun.

Special Events, Large and Small

Fun times can ease the day-to-day strain and refresh your family life. When you take a few minutes to think of fun things to do, all sorts of ideas start popping up.

Peek at this family's schedule: "Dinner time is when we spend time together. Sometimes it is more rushed than I would like because of homework that needs to be done. Saturdays generally are play days for the kids, and I clean house. Sundays we have church together, and we always follow it with a picnic. If it is too cold to go outside, we eat on a blanket on the floor in the living room. The kids love it almost as much as eating outside."

A weekly picnic woven into the daily busyness of life; what sorts of similar activities might you offer your children for family fun?

Celebrating Your Family Life

Have fun events built into your schedule. This way, the activities are more likely to happen. Sure, life can be serious. But recall again the familiar passage in Ecclesiastes 3:4: there is "a time to weep and a time to laugh, a time to mourn and a time to dance." Trouble will come your way, so make time for fun and games too.

Ask your children for suggestions. "We make it a point to plan events as a family, whether it's a vacation to the mountains or simply dinner at a restaurant," a father says. "One of the things I promised myself was that I would always 'know' my kids."

Allow yourself to be lighthearted. Sometimes we think we need to be serious or we feel that we have too many cares to let loose. Laugh with your children.

Time Together

Often the hardest part about having fun as a family is scheduling the time—time in the evenings, weekend hours, time off from work. This has to be worked around jobs and school, chores, and a host of obligations. You might think you do not have enough time or money to have fun as a family, but this is where creativity and simplicity come in.

Decide you are going to find a way to have more fun together. This requires an honest assessment of how well you have been doing, and what you might need to change. You probably will have to give up time doing something else in order to make this happen.

"While together, either out or at home, we always come up with family songs, sometimes funny sayings, and even a silly face that reminds us not to take all things too seriously, and that God's plan is for us to enjoy this life and our time here together," says one mother. Their family is known as "the family that entertains itself," and even their young daughter knows that makes them special.

"The key to having more fun together is being intentional," says a mother whom I often observe having great fun with her family. "If you're not intentional about it, then another day will pass, another week, another month, and what have you got to show for it? You'll wake up one day and realize that the kids are grown and that you missed your chance."

Begin to take steps that suit your family's life. Some people love the outdoors—camping, fishing, and hiking. Others like movies and games. Gather the family and make a list. You might ask each person to write down ten fun things your family could do for free. Then you might ask them to make a list of ten things you could do in your city or state, activities that might cost a little money but won't be outrageously expensive.

Look for small daily activities that can be fun, such as playing a sport in the yard or walking around the block.

"We spent a lot of one-on-one time practicing softball, especially when she was learning to pitch," one father says of his now-grown daughter. "My shins still have the scars! Even so, I would not trade that time for anything in the world."

"Make time for fun," says a mother whose children are also grown. "I was very task-oriented. In hindsight I should have made more time for fun. We went through a period of time when we had a 'family game night' every Friday evening. We ate something fun for dinner, played a game as a family, and had prizes for the winners and losers. I remember that as a fun time. We also got into a pattern of eating nachos and watching *America's Funniest Home Videos* on Sunday nights. That is a happy memory."

From another parent: "To the kids, a great night is often as simple as their father jumping on the trampoline with them for a while, or all of us playing a game of H-O-R-S-E at the basketball goal in the driveway, or playing cards before bed. Anybody can do those things. The hardest part of doing those things is putting aside the things you *think* you need to be doing (laundry, paying bills, cleaning house) and doing the things they will remember instead. I normally do those other things after the kids have gone to bed."

Make the most of special occasions. Everyone likes to feel special on his or her birthday, so look for ways to make birthdays a happy, fun occasion at your house. This doesn't mean that you have to have a big party, but make the birthday boy or birthday girl feel special. Let them know how much they're loved and how thankful you are that they were born.

Consider your children's likes and dislikes and their special personalities to plan occasions that mean the most to them. A story comes to mind here from a friend who once threw a big birthday party for her young son. "I wanted very much to teach my kids to socialize," she says. "My parents lacked in this department, and I resented it and wanted very much to give my children the chance to have a social life. So I always had big parties for them. My oldest son is introverted and gets overwhelmed when lots of people are around. I had a huge party at a horse ranch (that I'm pretty sure I couldn't afford) for him. He was completely overwhelmed. I realized about two years later that the party was more for me and what I wanted, rather than what was appropriate for a three-year-old."

Know your children, and keep in mind what is fun for them.

Develop unique family traditions. Take advantage of holidays and other times to do things that are meaningful to your family. Our family, like many, gathers for Thanksgiving, a day given to eating and visiting and playing. The cast includes cousins and grandchildren and grandnieces and grandnephews. This day has become extra enjoyable because everyone relaxes, we are not on much of a schedule, and we are ready for an enjoyable activity.

This past year, my niece, my granddaughter, and my second cousin corralled us all to watch their production of an original play with props that included various items pilfered from around our house. They announced it before lunch with a flyer they had created on the computer, and they handed out tickets that were required for entry into the "theater," which was actually our living room. Their written rules? "No wrestling, and no refreshments." (The latter rule caused a bit of an adult commotion with all that leftover pie and coffee!) On a previous Thanksgiving, the girls engineered a group jump rope extravaganza. Trying to remember old rhymes and avoiding seriously injuring ourselves brought enjoyment on that occasion to children from the age of two to adults at the age of eighty.

Schedule special events and activities to enrich the lives of children and grandchildren. If you are going to splurge on something, consider replacing more stuff with fun memories.

A retired friend and her husband focus on such activities with their out-of-state grandchildren. They have a long list of special things they do, including offering a special event for each birthday, taking their grandchildren to cultural events, and providing splurges such as a Christmastime train ride. "When my husband and I were growing up, the family was a priority, and we tried to make that true for our children as well," she says. "Now that the grandchildren are here, families are pulled in many directions. When the girls come to see us, they do not watch TV (which is our rule), but instead they play games, read, and cook. They love to be in the kitchen, and then we have time to interact, teach them how to plan meals, make a grocery list, and go to the store. In the summer, we join the library's reading club. Our hope is that these events will translate to memories as the years go by, and we knew that they would be special for us too."

Just hearing that family's list of fun activities makes me want to schedule a play date!

Vacation Time

Whether you can afford to take a big trip or need to plan an outing close by in the neighborhood, be sure to plan for time off. It is all too easy to get caught up in a 24/7 work schedule and neglect family fun time.

A major component of balancing home and work is taking time to refresh and renew, and the regrets parents express about this are intense. Put family time on the calendar. Discuss plans with your mate. You will be more effective at work if you recharge at home.

Look no further than to the book of Exodus for a reminder about taking time off: "Six days you shall do your work, but on the seventh day you shall rest, so that your ox and your donkey may have relief" (Exodus 23:12 NRSV). What a practical reminder that we probably need a little relief ourselves!

When Money Is Tight

Having fun together does not have to be expensive, but it may require a shift in attitude. Your family may expect an activity that costs money, such as going to a movie or eating out or taking a trip. Often, small things can be fun, such as riding bicycles together or playing football in the yard, or visiting a place of local interest somewhere in your own community. These kinds of activities build memories of closeness, and they cost little.

- "When we couldn't afford to take a big trip, we would take mini-vacations," says the mother of two grown children and two grandchildren. "On a Saturday, we would pack some sandwiches and head out, sometimes to gather fall leaves, other times just riding in the country until we saw somewhere we wanted to stop."
- Parents sometimes go overboard in an attempt to give children the experiences that they, as adults, did not have. "I think we have gone too far and have forgotten the simple pleasures of life that kids yearn for," says a father of three boys. "This sounds weird, but I pitched the tents and we camped in our backyard the other day—we made s'mores on the fire pit and sat around telling folk tales. The kids loved it, and so did I. It did not require any travel or preparation, and we bonded."
- A retired journalist still recalls the fun that her busy parents made time for: "Despite the many demands on my parents' time, they found ways for us to do things together as a family: play card games, go to summer band concerts, go sailing on the lake. Trips were best, because we children had our parents all to ourselves. We'd travel to Houston for Astros baseball games, to

Nebraska to visit family, to New York or Disneyland or the Grand Canyon. I still love the adventure of seeing new places and meeting new people."

Sacrificing Your Alone Time

You know that it is often difficult for parents to find time for everything that needs doing. Giving up something you want to do—whether it's a game of golf or a trip to the mall—may be necessary in order to find time for family fun.

"I have to try really hard not to be selfish," says a young father. "With the choice we made to bring a child into this world, we decided that sacrifices would have to be made. These sacrifices have been more than worth it, of course."

With and for Grandparents

As a grandmother, I have come to realize the importance of spending time with our granddaughter, no matter what. Since she lives 600 miles from us, visits can be a challenge, and we're always hungry for more fun times. At the start of each year, we try to negotiate weeks when she can visit, as we compare our calendars.

For those of you who juggle busy schedules that include other parents and grandparents, you know this sometimes is not easy. It helps to start planning as early as possible. For example, I go to my granddaughter's school district calendar online and mark key dates, such as her Christmas holidays and Spring Break, when school starts, and when it ends. This helps us plan around our work schedules, and it makes sure that we won't let too much time slip by without seeing our granddaughter.

127

When we have her with us, we try to enjoy that time with a mix of activities and relaxed visiting. A year or so ago, I had made plans for what I considered a big excursion. As I tucked my granddaughter in, I asked her, "Do you know what we're going to do tomorrow?" She looked up, delighted. "Play?" she asked. That was a learning moment for me. I think that sometimes we overplan and overdo, when an easy playtime would more than suffice.

As I write these words and look at a picture of my granddaughter and my niece sitting in a rocking chair on the porch of my office, I want to do more. This is a priority for me, and a blessing that adds so much to life.

Whether you are a young parent who wants to help your children build a strong relationship with your parents, or a grandparent who would like to have more fun with the grandchildren, look for ways to help and have fun at the same time, and look at this as part of your ongoing parenting journey. Listen to how some grandparents describe their efforts:

- "With my daughters, who are now in their thirties, I pushed them to be their best in everything they did. Looking back on it, I wish I had relaxed more and let them relax more. They both turned out great, so I was just lucky. With my grandchildren, I want them to be happy and enjoy their lives. I am relaxed, and I just try to have fun with them. Sure, we read and have 'educational moments,' but we concentrate more on life's lessons and on enjoying each moment as it comes."

- "Speaking as a long-distance grandparent, it's challenging to stay connected. It's a balancing act. It takes physical energy, balancing the budget, logistical planning, scheduling with work, and gasoline," says one mother and grandmother. She and her children use a common calendar online to keep up with one another's big events, and they are intentional about scheduling get-togethers. "Planning, planning, planning, and budgeting too" go into her efforts.

- "When I visit, my plans are to spend as much time with my toddler grandson as I can. I let his mom and dad sleep in, and I get him dressed, take him to eat breakfast, and then head to the park."
- "We have a responsibility to create memories with our grandchildren. Forget about what the neighbors might think when you're playing hide-and-seek in the front yard, using a flashlight on a cloudy day, or wearing weeds in your buttonholes or hair. We may never know what kind of impact we have on our grandchildren."
- "We always look forward to the grandchildren visiting and are tired when they leave. But we hope their time with us will make a difference in the long term."

Having Fun with Other Family Members

As you draw up lists of fun family activities, look for ways to help your children connect in joyful ways with other relatives—cousins, aunts and uncles, and, of course, grandparents. If you think back on Bible stories, you'll recall Christ celebrating at a wedding, families gathering regularly for meals, and deep connections between relatives. So many times these days, you'll hear families at funerals lamenting that they do not get together except when tragedy or sadness, such as the death of a loved one, occurs. Try instead to build family traditions and get-togethers into your fun times.

One mother who makes time for her extended family has

a list of ways she helps her children grow through those relationships:

- showing respect with good manners;
- visiting their homes;
- doing special outings with them;
- calling them and getting the children to talk; and
- sending pictures.

She and an aunt and other family members get together for holidays and for a summer trip, when all the cousins get together and play. "When you make memories like that, it's a bonding time," she says.

A cousin was determined to get my mother's side of the family together. She pushed and prodded and pulled us together at her farm for great food and visiting. I see so clearly the beautiful fall day when we gathered outside for a huge potluck and gabfest. The small children were swinging on a tire swing, and two girls were lying in a hammock, sharing secrets of their lives 200 miles apart. We need this connection and reminder of who we are and where we came from.

Look for ways to connect your children with aunts and uncles when possible. Because I married relatively "late," I spent lots of time with my nieces and nephews, and my life has been enriched in so many ways, as I have watched them grow and start families of their own.

"I have such great memories of my aunts," a longtime friend says. "There were my great-aunts who hand-stitched a complete Barbie wardrobe for me when I was little. I still have all the clothes, down to the tiny white gloves. I think aunts can fill in where sometimes parents can't. They really add another dimension to the family."

Even as an adult, her life is enhanced by these relationships. She tells this story of a lunch with aunts and uncles: "We lingered at the dining table a long time and told lots of funny stories and shared things. Mom pulled out a scrapbook that Dad had kept of stuff from when he was a young coach and from when he was a high school and junior college star football player. It sure made me wish Dad could have been there to tell some stories, which he was always so good at."

Those types of relationships can help shape your family in untold ways. As a young dad says of his baby daughter, "I want her to look back at her family—her extended family—and to know how much she has been loved throughout her life. I want her to know how many lives she has touched by being here with us."

Maybe you want to find new ways to make memories. One mother puts a premium on this, saying, "Memories are about making the littlest things worth remembering. I want my kids to appreciate the small things, and not to keep looking for memories to come from things that come along only once in a while. Everyday things make wonderful memories, from creating a movie night with your family and friends, to sharing popcorn and ice cream sandwiches, to lying in bed at night with your children telling stories."

Whatever you do, however busy you are, make time for fun. Everyone knows the truth that time goes so quickly. Have fun as a family. You won't regret it.

Questions to Consider as You Go Forward

- What fun things does your family enjoy?
- What is a favorite memory of having a good time together?

- What makes your family laugh?

A PRAYER FOR YOUR JOURNEY

Dear Lord, please bring more joy into my daily life and my family time. Show me what to embrace and celebrate. Help me slow down and have fun. Thank you for your gifts and for the abundant life you offer so generously. Help me seize that life and savor it; in the wonderful name of Christ. Amen.

Observations from Busy Families

"Don't spend the time when your children are awake doing housework. Save those necessary but mundane things for when they are asleep. If that is the only time you have, then make sure you are sharing the time with your children anyway. If they are doing homework and you are folding laundry, make sure you are doing it in the same room."

"Family nights are a great way to slow down. This time brings the family together, and the kids get a break from their friends."

"Love them by spending time with them, doing things together, rather than by unlimited amounts of material goods. Children want you to spend time with them versus buying them stuff all the time."

Quick Tip

"Have a picnic in the den. Make ordinary days fun."

Chapter Ten

FINDING TIME FOR YOU

Encouraging Word: *You will have more time to offer your family if you allow time for yourself.*
Everyday Step: *Block out a few minutes of alone time each day.*

I urge you to live a life worthy of the calling
you have received. Be completely humble and gentle;
be patient, bearing with one another in love.
—Ephesians 4:1-2

An oxygen mask on an airplane seems like an odd symbol to remind busy parents of their everyday responsibilities, but it is the best I've heard. An extremely busy working mother offers this insight: "I often think of the airplane analogy. If you are on a plane and it runs into trouble, you are advised to cover your mouth with the oxygen mask and to begin breathing through it first, *before* you try to help others. It goes completely against everything we ever believe to take care of ourselves first. However, if we do not, we cannot take care of others. Parents must know what works for them, what helps them to recharge. So often nowadays people do not even know themselves well enough to know what they like to do as a break to recharge."

133

With time in short supply, grown-up activities seem hardest of all to make happen. Some parents feel guilty when they do things for themselves. Spare minutes are given to the children. Spouses and friends are neglected. Others have gotten so wrapped up in their children's lives that they hardly recognize themselves anymore. They *used* to have hobbies and date nights, but what was that all about? Now they feel as though they don't deserve time alone or couldn't possibly work it in.

Learning to schedule time for yourself and your spouse is an integral part of having a less-hurried and less-worried family. When you do so, you will return to your children refreshed. You will be more creative and have new ideas. Little things won't bug you quite so much.

Yes, your children need you. But they don't have to have you *all* of the time. You probably don't even need instructions on finding time for yourself. You simply need to be reminded why it matters.

You can't do it all. In fact, do you even *want* to?

The responsibility of being a parent demands a lot, but it is not all-or-nothing every minute of every day. Find your middle ground, and ease up on occasion.

Be heartened by 2 Corinthians 12:9: "My grace is sufficient for you, for my power is made perfect in weakness."

A Little Time Each Day

Often bedtime rolls around, and we are amazed. "Where did the day go?"

Carve out even a sliver of quiet time each day. Make this a time when you pray or write in your journal or read or listen to music you like. This can help you pay attention not only to your own spirit, but to God's guidance for your family.

134

You may find that you have been ignoring something that needs action, or neglecting an important issue.

Even if you have little extra time each day, find a few minutes for you, and find something that gives you energy.

Take a deep breath.

Offer thanks for the good of the day, and collect yourself. Here is a tender reminder: "Give thanks to the LORD, for he is good; / his love endures forever" (1 Chronicles 16:34). Saying thanks again and again, and listing the many good things in each day can renew you immediately.

Focus on having more time for things you really enjoy, adult activities, no children allowed! Maybe this means a hobby you used to love or exercising or visiting with friends. Perhaps it will include spending more time with your spouse, having fun and reconnecting.

Have a set bedtime for your children. This can allow time for yourself in the evening. "I usually spend 9:00 until 11:00 by myself to prepare for the next day, check personal e-mail, and so on," says one mother. "I also reserve a few specific days to watch my favorite shows. That helps me relax."

Live with Contentment

Give thought to these questions to help renew yourself as a parent and partner, and to refresh your mind, body, and soul:

- What gives me energy?
- What drains my energy?
- How can I add more energy to my life?
- What do I need to cut from my life?
- What happens when I ignore self-care?
- What do I do differently when I take care of myself?

Taking care of yourself is not something you are doing only for you, although you deserve it. You also do it to have the energy you need for your children, your spouse, and your job, to become the person you were created to be and to find ways to use your special talents and gifts. Seize this reminder from the Old Testament: "I have loved you with an everlasting love; / I have drawn you with loving-kindness" (Jeremiah 31:3).

As you travel through this part of your journey, you may find it hard at first to squeeze in a moment or two for you. Keep calling upon God. One of the most inspiring Bible verses for me is Ephesians 3:20, where we are told that the Lord "is able to do immeasurably more than all we ask or imagine, according to his power that is at work within us." "*Immeasurably more*"! That includes helping you manage your time.

If you are constantly on the go and worrying about other people, you will have a tough time listening to yourself. You may ignore important messages, pushing down that uneasy feeling in your stomach. You could overlook God's plan for your life or neglect a needed change.

Some of the joy of being a parent can slip away, making you feel like a martyr or chauffeur, or taken for granted and put upon. As you refresh, you will grow in contentment. "I have learned to be content whatever the circumstances," the Apostle Paul says in Philippians 4:11. In taking time for yourself, you will discover new ways to cope with tough times and find new energy for tiring days.

Remember Those Seasons of Time?

The time you find for yourself—or for your spouse—will depend on many things. The ages of your children, how much time you are away for work, whether you have friends or relatives close by to babysit or whether you can afford to pay a sitter; all these come into play.

A pat formula for renewal obviously won't work. Once again, you have to figure out what works for you. Believe that you can find time here and there to recharge your battery. While there may be periods of life when you long for a weekend away but know it will not come, you can almost always find *some* time. Keep dreaming and looking for ways to be refreshed right where you are.

Make a list of ten things you would like to do for fun, just for you, or for you and your spouse.

Choose one thing from your list and schedule it within the next three months.

Know what your priorities for free time are. For example, one single mother carves out time for a midweek prayer group that is important to her. She also hires a babysitter if there is something she really likes to do, such as dinner or a movie with friends. When you become more certain about how you want to use even small amounts of free time, you are less likely to fritter those moments away doing something you don't enjoy.

Make time for exercise. This can improve your health, increase your energy, and lessen your stress. While it may be difficult to build the habit, start small. Take a stroll in the evenings, or get up earlier than the rest of the family and jump rope or start jogging. Find what is right for you, and do it.

"I work out regularly," says a mother whose children are old enough to stay alone for a little while. "The way I accomplish that is, when we walk in the door, I give the kids a goal of forty-five minutes or an hour and say, 'When I get back in from working out, I want you to have your homework finished and

your baths taken, and then we will . . .' whatever *it* may be."
This allows her time to have a good walk in the neighborhood,
and it motivates them to get their chores done so that they can
enjoy the evening together.

**Consider hobbies you used to have or activities you
enjoyed.** Why did you give them up? How might you begin
to weave them into your life? For example, perhaps you liked
running or cycling. Could you make time for such activities
by getting up earlier and doing them while the children are
still asleep? Such an activity might be worth the sacrifice of
some sleep.

**Talk with your spouse about scheduling time for the two
of you.** You don't have to start with something major. Plan a
date night, or a movie, or dinner at a non-fast-food restaurant, somewhere you actually eat with a fork and knife!

"Our philosophy is first to make sure that our marriage is
healthy in every aspect," says a husband of twenty-three
years and father of teens. "We continue to go out on dates
and to spend quality time with each other. It is our belief that
if we build our marriage, then our children will have a great
example of how a relationship between husband and wife
should be."

Plan a weekend with friends. Go on a road trip with
friends, and leave the cares of home behind for a couple of
days. Ask your spouse to take care of the home front, and
trade off for time away for him or her.

Give Your Spouse a Break

Do not begrudge your spouse a chance to renew, and do
not feel as though you never get to do anything. As a new
father says, "Don't be selfish with your time. Everyone wants
and needs alone time, but realize that you aren't the only one

who feels that way. Remember that your spouse also wants and needs to get away sometimes."

Make it easy for your spouse to have a fun weekend. Encourage him or her to do so, and don't complain when the time for it rolls around. Learn to give and take. Don't grumble, and don't whine.

While you're at it, back each other up day by day. "I am a hurry-less and worry-less kind of guy," says one father. "But as a family, we compensate for each other. My wife usually does all of the hurrying and worrying. If I hurry and worry some, my wife worries less, and vice versa. The less I worry and the less I do, the more my wife worries and hurries." Help each other out. Make this sort of give-and-take part of the daily flow.

Ask for Help from Others

Plan times when family or friends can help out. Ask for their help. Offer to trade babysitting with them or to keep their children for an evening. Let others know when you need a break. While spontaneous dates might be nice, they may be harder to make happen, especially if you have young children. Pull out your calendar and start working on making something happen down the road. Not only will you have an adult play date on the schedule, you will have something to look forward to.

For grandparents: be aware of your children's lives and offer to help them out, rather than making them ask. As my friend says of her adult daughter who lives in another state, "I can tell when she needs her mama."

Times of Retreat

I lead many retreats, and I love watching people start to relax over the course of only a couple of days. You do not have to step away from society for weeks on end to feel the healing power of renewal. It's amazing how difficult it is for people to step away for a weekend, though. When they first arrive, they are often exhausted with the effort of getting out of town, and they may be feeling a bit guilty for all they have left behind. It takes a while for them to shift gears and begin to slow down.

The value of these retreats is that they give busy parents time to step back and consider what they are doing. They offer time to reflect and rest. They help people clear their minds. They can help you determine if you are thinking big enough for your own life and your family's; if you're limiting God or neglecting a dream or vision you once had for yourself and your children.

Be open to opportunities to retreat in your life, such as a workshop offered by your church or by an organization in your area. Give yourself permission to go. Once you are there, give yourself permission to put thoughts of home away for a bit and to regain your energy and focus.

Even if you don't have time to get away, keep in mind tips that can help you recharge. Here is a simple list to refer to when you need a boost:

- Take a deep breath. Feel God's love surrounding you.
- Consider the many good things in your life. Give thanks.
- Be amazed at how many gifts you have to offer to the world.
- Make up your mind to enjoy today. Don't worry about yesterday. Don't fret about tomorrow. Enjoy today.
- Pray for God's guidance and blessings.
- Hurry less. Slow it down.
- Worry less. Be anxious for nothing.
- Look for the best in each situation and in each person. Say "good-bye" to Murphy's Law—the belief that anything that *can* go wrong *will* go wrong.

- Simplify your plans.
- Learn to say no. Always know that when you say no to one thing, you say yes to something else.
- Get a good night's sleep.
- Exercise. Take a walk around the block or around the yard.
- Enjoy nature. Get outside more often. Observe the seasons.
- Read.
- Keep a journal.
- Just do your best. Let some things go.
- Remember that you are God's creation!

Christ as Your Model

Perhaps you still feel guilty about even considering stepping back or taking some time away. Consider the most wonderful model of this: Christ our Lord. Jesus had a lot that he needed to do—sermons to preach, people to heal. Every time he turned around, someone was touching his garment for healing or begging for help.

Yet Jesus always took time to step back. He went away to pray. He withdrew from the crowd. He drew a few people close around him for support. I do not believe for a moment that Christ did not intend for us to do likewise.

The Sabbath was even included in the Ten Commandments. That is a time of worship and rest and joy, a time to step back from the work of everyday life.

Many parents have demanding jobs. These jobs are hard either physically or mentally or emotionally, or all three. If you do not allow yourself to take time to recover from some of those strains, your family likely will suffer. A physician says that he becomes "a bit reclusive when my brain is too full. Thinking of things I like doing helps to reset me. It makes my home life richer when I 're-enter.' "

Reflect on these words from a mother, and see if they might help you do things differently: "I have a great passion for my work. However, that passion can be draining at the same time. It is hard to turn it off when I go home, hard not to think about and worry about the people I serve. I recharge in a number of ways. I pray daily for the people I serve, for myself and for my family, and for those around me. I am thankful and grateful to God for my life and for the many blessings I have been given through grace alone. I attend church regularly and am committed to my church's work in our community. I make it a point to connect with those who are dearest to me, my friends and family, both here and 'back home.' I call, e-mail, send handwritten notes to friends, and visit when I can. This helps me remember who I am and why I do the work I do each day. I write in my journal daily. I have lunch with friends and spend time talking about stuff other than work. I take time out to have a manicure. A couple of times a year I treat myself to a massage. There are many small things I do, when I feel the stress is overwhelming, just to take a timeout and recharge myself."

As a family, allow time when the children are the focus, and have great experiences—and make sure you have times when Mom and Dad get away, if only for an hour or two.

Give Yourself a Break, and Give Thanks

Being a parent may be the most wonderful and most difficult job in the world. Regularly step back to say thanks for the honor, and even for the challenges. Ease up on yourself a bit, and don't expect perfection from yourself or from your children. Step back when you need to, and get up and go again.

Figure out what you need and want to do as a parent. Be encouraged by the words of other parents on the same journey.

You don't have to figure it all out at once. Keep trying. "Not that I have already obtained all this," the Bible tells us, "or have already been made perfect, but I press on to take hold of that for which Christ Jesus took hold of me" (Philippians 3:12).

Turn to God for support and wisdom, and for help in your daily life. Remember these words from Christ in John 14:27: "Peace I leave with you; my peace I give you. I do not give to you as the world gives. Do not let your hearts be troubled and do not be afraid."

Your family is unique. Identify changes you want and need. Focus on what is important. Make decisions accordingly. Life flows past us, always changing, ever unfolding. You will make mistakes. You'll need to stop and get your bearings. Your children will grow and will seem like different creatures from time to time.

When you look back, you will be glad that you made the effort to hurry less and worry less.

Questions to Consider as You Go Forward

- How might you find a few minutes each day to be alone?
- What is a fun activity you could do with a friend?
- How might you and your spouse find more time to enjoy together?

A PRAYER FOR YOUR JOURNEY

Dear Lord, I seek time to be refreshed and renewed. Help me slow down and catch my breath. Show me how to balance time for fun with my family, with time for fun for myself. Teach me ways to take better care of myself. Thank you for the guidance you offer and for the gift of life; in your name. Amen.

Observations from Busy Families

"*Keep trying;* people tell me it matters. I'm right in the middle of this, but older parents keep telling me that, and it does help keep me going."

"Take time to enjoy many small things, even while planning grand things."

"I made a career change because I felt I was ready to explore new adventures. I just felt I needed to continue to see what was out there. I kept feeling, and still do, that there is so much more I want to do in life. You can't let fear keep you from doing it."

Quick Tip

"Stop thinking that you have to fix everything."

Study Guide

*Delight yourself in the LORD / and he will give you the
desires of your heart.*
—Psalm 37:4

Hurry Less, Worry Less for Families can be used for individual reflection or as a guide for group study, to help you in your efforts toward having a loving, joyful family. The perspectives of many different parents throughout this book offer starting points for thought and discussion.

Using the book's ten chapters as an outline, this study guide provides for each chapter:

- a key point to consider;
- a reflection on a Bible passage;
- reflection/discussion questions;
- a step to take in the week ahead.

With Scripture passages woven throughout the text, this book can help readers learn more about the Bible and how to incorporate biblical teachings into everyday life. Incorporating renewal time into daily life is one way to hurry less and worry less within the family, and this study guide can help you start a habit of prayer and reflection. In addition, individual readers can answer each chapter's questions in a journal or a notebook during a quiet time, while group members can use the questions to shape conversation.

This study invites participation, but it also focuses on each individual's family journey and is suited for a diverse group. Each of us is uniquely created, and we are at different places in our family lives. This means that responses to questions may be very personal and may vary greatly. This study can also help a group develop as a community. It can help family members discover the next steps on their journey. It is suitable for Sunday school, vacation Bible school, or a small group.

Suggestions for Individual Study

Personal study time is helpful, but it can be hard to maintain. Using a book such as this one as a guide can be useful. Consider using a journal or a notebook as you move through the book, jotting down your ideas and pondering how God might be speaking to you each day. A journal can be a very helpful tool as you sort your thoughts. You can also use it to list prayer requests, note things you are thankful for, and write down prayers.

Many of us get bogged down for a variety of reasons during individual study time. The most common reason is that it's hard to find study time in our busy, noisy lives. I encourage you to set aside time to read a chapter of the book and then to reflect upon it.

Start or Join a Small Group

This book will work well for a group of parents or grandparents, and such a group can add richness to your life, providing you with people from whom you can learn, and with whom you can grow and have fun. These groups often become like a loving family, helping one another in tough times and celebrating together in good times. While group meetings do not replace individual quiet time, they add a new perspective to study.

How do you find such a group? If you attend church, ask at the church office or take a look at the church's website. If you have not found a church to call home, ask friends or coworkers.

If you have been involved in a church or a Bible study, you might want to consider *starting* a new small group. Pray about this, and you will be amazed at how your group might form. Often a church staff member will know of people who are interested in a new group, and organizing it can be an astonishing ministry. This is a good way to serve and to use such gifts as teaching, leadership, and hospitality. Perhaps you can help other parents on their journey.

Remember: you do not have to be a preacher or a Bible scholar to lead a small group. You simply have to help pull the group together, encourage others, and be yourself. If you feel called to lead a group, then prepare in advance for each class. Write down an agenda for the meeting in order to keep on track, and use notes as needed. Notify group members where you will be meeting, and when. Encourage group participation, but do not try to force anyone to talk. Pray each week for an awareness of God's presence in the midst of your group.

Reminders for Group Leaders

This book can be used as a ten-week study with one chapter for each week, or as a six-week study, starting with an introductory discussion and covering two chapters in each of the following weeks. It can also work for a vacation Bible school class. A suggested approach for four nights would be to cover the introduction and the first two chapters on night one; chapters 3 through 5 on night two; chapters 6 through 8 on night three; and chapters 9 and 10 on night four.

Each session can last from one hour to an hour-and-a-half or even longer, depending on the amount of time you allow for discussion. Participants should read the chapters in advance if possible to prepare for the discussion and to enable them to think about how God is speaking in their lives.

To get your meeting space ready, add touches to make it more personal and comfortable. Consider adding a candle, for example, and perhaps a cross, flowers, or an item symbolic of the week's discussion. You might ask group members to help with such items, making this a participatory activity. For example, you might ask participants to bring photos of their family to serve as reminders of the heart of this study.

Be available early to greet people when they arrive and to welcome visitors. Some groups enjoy taking turns bringing snacks or a light meal. This practice can help build a close spirit within the group and help newcomers relax as the group gathers.

Open each session with prayer, asking for God's presence in guiding the discussion. Allow people to share in the conversation, but avoid making it seem as though someone *has* to speak. As the weeks unfold, you likely will find that group members are more eager to open up. Remind your group that class discussions are confidential. And make sure that each person has pen and paper available for taking notes.

A Sample Session

- Open with prayer and casual conversation, and provide time for chatting as participants settle in.
- Direct participants to "Going a Step Further," below, using this as an outline for the class. Ask if anyone has

comments or questions on discussions from previous meetings.

- As the meeting begins, focus on the main scripture for each chapter.
- Begin your discussion with the "Key Point to Consider."
- Lead the group in reading and discussing the "Reflection/Discussion Questions."
- In each chapter, ask group members to choose a step they will take during the coming week, and invite them to reflect on their thoughts during the course of the week.
- Mention which chapters should be read before the next meeting.
- You might want to invite prayer requests as the session ends. Pray for God's guidance as each class member seeks to follow God's will and enrich family life.

Going a Step Further: Reflection/Discussion Questions for Groups or Individuals

After reading each chapter, reflect upon the scripture identified in the study guide, turn to the "Key Point to Consider," and ponder what it means in your life. Use the "Reflection/ Discussion Questions" to go a step further and help you sense how God is leading. Sometimes one question will lead to a discussion that takes you into the next, or a particular topic will jump out at you. Let the Spirit guide you to spend time as needed with these questions and to reframe them to be most effective. Individual needs within a group can be powerful in shaping discussions.

Each chapter ends with a "Focus on Growth," a step you might take to make changes in your family life or to deepen your faith. This is a step that you identify and commit to take, custom-made to help you move forward with joy. Remember that God is calling you and your unique family to do special things with your life. God wants you to live abundantly and to find meaning and joy within and among your family. Each person, each family, is different, so ask what God's will is for your life and your family—and what steps you might take to be transformed in your faith, individually and together, so that you might experience family more fully. Pray about your answers, and let God shape your life.

Study Guide

Chapter 1

A Fresh Look at Your Family

Key Point to Consider: Step back and consider your family with new eyes. Focus on what is most important to you and how you can make daily decisions that support those priorities.

Reflect on the Scripture: "Ask and it will be given to you; seek and you will find; knock and the door will be opened to you" (Luke 11:9). What does this verse mean in your family's life?

Reflection/Discussion Questions

1. Chapter 1 points out that many parents expect too much of themselves. What evidence of this do you see in your life?
2. How might you change your thinking to be more realistic and yet continue to grow as a parent?
3. What are you doing *right* as a parent? What would you like to change?
4. As you consider asking God for help each day, in what area do you most need that guidance?
5. One parent mentions making mistakes and struggling to maintain a proper balance. Are there similarities with this parent's experience in your own life? If so, in what ways? What do you see as keys to maintaining balance in life?

Focus on Growth: Decide on a step you will take in the week ahead to make your family life more joyful.

Chapter 2

Enough Time to Go Around

Key Point to Consider: You have enough time to enjoy your family, but you may have to adjust your priorities and cut something from your schedule. Children, too, need help choosing activities and avoiding getting overloaded.

Reflect on the Scripture: "Yet this I call to mind / and therefore I have hope: / Because of the LORD's great love we are not consumed, / for his compassions never fail. / They are new every morning" (Lamentations 3:21-23). What do these verses mean to you?

Reflection/Discussion Questions

1. Chapter 2 mentions the importance of knowing what your priorities are, and deciding how those look in your daily life. On what key priorities would you most like to focus?
2. What keeps you from spending time on your priorities?
3. What might you trim from your schedule to allow more time for family?
4. Are your children or grandchildren too busy with activities? Is there a way you might help them slow down?
5. List three steps that can simplify your daily schedule.

Focus on Growth: Decide on one activity that you will eliminate from your schedule in the week ahead.

Chapter 3

The Rhythm of Home

Key Point to Consider: A slower daily routine and a weekly plan can make your home calmer and your family more relaxed. Home can become a cozy shelter where your family is safe and happy, and your routine is one that works for the entire family.

Reflect on the Scripture: "Even youths grow tired and weary, / and young men stumble and fall; / but those who hope in the LORD / will renew their strength" (Isaiah 40:30-31a). What do these verses say about family life?

Reflection/Discussion Questions

1. Chapter 3 says that having a good daily routine can make a big difference in slowing your family down. Why is it difficult to establish such a routine?
2. What parts of your daily and weekly routine work well? What parts need adjustment?
3. What is your family's favorite time at home?
4. Many families emphasize the importance of eating dinner together each evening. Why do you think they make this a priority? What is the importance of gathering for meals?
5. Families have different "seasons of time," depending on the ages of the children and other circumstances. How would you describe the "season of time" your family is in?

Focus on Growth: Decide on one step you will take in the week ahead to change your family's routine for the better.

Study Guide

Chapter 4

Organize to Energize

Key Point to Consider: Home can be a special place where families relax and have fun. Having an organized and tidy home requires everyone's participation and cooperation.

Reflect on the Scripture: "Look to the LORD and his strength; / seek his face always" (1 Chronicles 16:11). What might this verse suggest for your life?

Reflection/Discussion Questions

1. Chapter 4 mentions that most people want their houses to be more organized. Do you have tricks that help you get rid of clutter at home? If so, what are they? If not, what might you try?
2. How would you describe your family's personality? In what ways does your house reflect that?
3. One working mother describes how she plans chores in advance. In what way might you use a list and a plan to be more efficient at home?
4. Lots of families wrestle with homework each day. What sort of homework arrangements do you have at home or did you have when your children were in school? What works?
5. Technology offers new advantages as well as new challenges for families. How do you think computer use should be handled within the home? Do you think television watching should be limited?

Focus on Growth: Decide on one thing you can do regularly to keep clutter from accumulating at home.

Study Guide

Chapter 5

A Foundation of Faith

Key Point to Consider: A strong faith and commitment to God's guidance makes a huge difference for your family. Attending church regularly can help your children grow spiritually.

Reflect on the Scripture: "If anyone is thirsty, let him come to me and drink. Whoever believes in me, as the Scripture has said, streams of living water will flow from within him," (John 7:37-38). What does this verse tell you about faith for a family?

Reflection/Discussion Questions

1. Chapter 5 says that a commitment to faith, worship, and church involvement does not "just happen." Has that been true in your own life? Why do you think people have difficulties making church attendance part of their lives?
2. Sometimes children or a spouse do not want to attend church. What are some ways to deal with this?
3. Churches often help people during tough times in their lives. Have you ever experienced this? If so, how? What do you think the church's role is in helping families?
4. Serving others is part of our calling, but volunteering can add to an already busy schedule. How do you decide where to offer your time and energy?
5. How can teaching children to pray help them with their daily lives? Why is it sometimes difficult to lead children spiritually?

Focus on Growth: Decide on one thing you will do in the week ahead to help your children or grandchildren know that faith is important.

Study Guide

Chapter 6

Balancing Home and Work

Key Point to Consider: The demands of work often cause parents stress, but simple strategies can help you allow time for family even while holding a job. Each family is different and must make hard choices about jobs and finances.

Reflect on the Scripture: "I can do everything through him who gives me strength" (Philippians 4:13). In what ways can this verse give a parent hope in daily life?

Reflection/Discussion Questions

1. Chapter 6 says that many people work because they are *called* to their job, while others believe they are not to work outside the home. How have you dealt with this in your own life?
2. Parents often want to make more time for their children but find that work interferes. What are the results of this inner conflict?
3. Sometimes it is hard for a parent to attend a child's activities. How have you handled this in your own life? What tips might you offer another parent?
4. Some parents remain in jobs they do not enjoy. What are some reasons individuals do this? What is your idea of having a healthy perspective on work and its place in life?
5. What should two-parent families consider when deciding whether one parent will stay at home or work part-time? What advice would you give to a single parent who is concerned with balancing the demands of parenthood and work?

Focus on Growth: List one way you will juggle your work better in the week ahead.

Chapter 7

When Hard Times Come Along

Key Point to Consider: Families frequently encounter rough times—illness, death, divorce, financial setbacks, discipline problems, and other challenges. Excessive worrying about family life can erode your joy and drain your energy. God's help is with you through bad times.

Reflect on the Scripture: "I cry aloud to the LORD; / I lift up my voice to the LORD for mercy. / I pour out my complaint before him; / before him I tell my trouble. / When my spirit grows faint within me, / it is you who know my way" (Psalm 142:1-3a). How do these verses speak to the tough times of life?

Reflection/Discussion Questions

1. Chapter 7 quotes a young parent who struggles not to worry about his child. Have you faced this same issue? If so, in what ways have you handled it? What is your advice for finding peace of mind regarding your family and their care?
2. One family specialist says that hardships can bring a family together. How might this be true?
3. Many parents must care not only for their children but also for their own aging parents. How might friends and family help in such situations?
4. Many families worry about money. In what ways might parents deal with their money-related concerns?

5. The Bible says not to be anxious about anything. Why is this so hard? How might you give up your worries to God?

Focus on Growth: Choose a worry that you will give up for the week ahead.

Chapter 8

The Simplicity of Consistency

Key Point to Consider: Children need consistency and appropriate discipline, but it is often hard for parents to say no to their kids. Sometimes, despite the best intentions, communication breaks down. Parents need to let their children know what is expected of them. Also, children need to consistently feel loved.

Reflect on the Scripture: "Train a child in the way he should go, / and when he is old he will not turn from it" (Proverbs 22:6). How does this verse guide parents in today's world?

Reflection/Discussion Questions

1. Chapter 8 tells about a young working mother who strives for more structure in her children's lives. She likes such structure in some ways, but it also makes her feel as though she is being too strict. How might parents handle this tension?
2. How can being too busy lead to discipline problems?
3. Why is it so difficult to tell children no? In what ways can saying no help a child?
4. Parents are sometimes concerned about how to love their child without being their child's "friend." Have

you seen this as an issue? If so, explain. Why do you think this could be a challenge?

5. In the Ten Commandments, having respect for your parents is listed. Why is it important that children respect their parents? Do you think this changes as children grow into adults? Why or why not?

Focus on Growth: Decide on a new or improved way to communicate with your family in the week ahead.

Chapter 9

Fun and Games

Key Point to Consider: Many parents want to have more fun with their children, and many regret the times they have let slip away. Fun times can build family relationships and ease the strain of daily life.

Reflect on the Scripture: "This is the day the LORD has made; / let us rejoice and be glad in it" (Psalm 118:24). How can this verse apply to enjoying family life more?

Reflection/Discussion Questions

1. Chapter 9 mentions how difficult it can be to schedule time for family fun. Why might this be the case? How might that be changed?

2. One mother discusses how quickly life passes and the importance of making family memories. How can a parent make this a priority?

3. Many families tell stories of happy times even when money was tight or recall special traditions that didn't

cost much money. What simple-but-fun family activities can you recall from your childhood?

4. Why is the role of grandparents and other relatives important in the lives of children? What memories of your grandparents or other older adults do you have? What did you learn from them?

5. List three reasons why it is important to have fun as a family.

Focus on Growth: Choose one fun thing you will be certain to do with your family in the week ahead.

Chapter 10

Finding Time for You

Key Point to Consider: Parents have more to offer their families if they allow time for renewing themselves. Learning to carve out time for yourself can be difficult but rewarding.

Reflect on the Scripture: "I urge you to live a life worthy of the calling you have received. Be completely humble and gentle; be patient, bearing with one another in love" (Ephesians 4:1-2). What guidelines do these verses offer for busy parents?

Reflection/Discussion Questions

1. Chapter 10 says that parents often give up doing things they enjoy because they feel guilty. Why is this so? In what ways can stepping back from daily life help a parent?

2. How can you make more time for self-care? What might happen if you cared more for yourself?
3. List a handful of things you would like to do for fun. How could you work some of those things into your schedule?
4. Parents often need help from others. Do you find it hard to ask for help? Why or why not? Is there someone who needs your help with his or her family? What can you do to offer help to such a person in need?
5. Why do you think Christ made prayer and rest time part of his routine? How might you learn from that?

Focus on Growth: List a step for renewal that you will take in the week ahead.

Tell Me Your Story

I would love to hear about your journey and your family. E-mail me at judy@judychristie.com. For ongoing tips on living fully, go to judychristie.com. Remember: Your family life can be a special joy. Don't let the days slip by in a blur!